Art Treasures of the Rijksmuseum

Art Treasures of the

RIJKSMUSEUM

Amsterdam

Foreword by A.F.E. van Schendel
Director General, The Rijksmuseum, Amsterdam

Texts by B. Haak
Member of the Curatorial Staff

Harry N. Abrams, Inc., Publishers, New York

Translated by Elizabeth Willems-Treeman

Designed by Wim Crouwel

Library of Congress Catalog Card Number: 66–10326

Printed and bound in the Netherlands

Contents

List of Plates

Foreword

Aerial View of the Rijksmuseum

Rijksmuseum means National Museum. In the Netherlands there are over a
dozen other state-owned museums, some of great importance, but only the
national museum in Amsterdam is called "the Rijksmuseum" without
further designation, indicating its unique position. At home and abroad the
word Rijksmuseum stands for a treasure house of the highest artistic
achievements of the Dutch, especially in the field of painting. The Low
Countries are considered to have found in painting the most universal expression
of their particular genius in the arts. And the Rijksmuseum is always
associated with the names of those who most strongly embodied this genius in
their masterpieces—Rembrandt, Vermeer, Frans Hals, and many others.
This has been so for over a hundred and fifty years. The Rijksmuseum belongs
among the earliest national museums in the world, its history going back to the
period following the French Revolution. In 1795 the French occupied
Holland, drove out the Stadholder, Prince William V of Orange, and, with the
help of the anti-Orange party among the Dutch, set up the Batavian Republic.
As one result of this revolution, part of the Stadholder's collections was sent
to Paris, and another part was publicly sold. But numerous paintings and
objects of historic interest were left in the residences of the Orange family.
These works were brought together in the Huis ten Bosch, the summer
palace near The Hague, where as early as 1800 the National Art Gallery was
opened to the public.
This art gallery was the precursor of the Rijksmuseum. In 1806 the Batavian
Republic became the Kingdom of Holland, Napoleon Bonaparte having
placed his liberal-minded brother Louis Napoleon on the throne. Louis soon
began to interest himself in the art collection and directed that plans be made
for the foundation of a royal museum. He decided to transfer the royal
residence from Utrecht to Amsterdam, where the Town Hall on the Dam
was put at his disposal as palace. From there, on April 21, 1808 (the day after
he moved in), he issued a decree establishing the Grand Musée Royal.
Cornelis Apostool, consular agent and amateur painter, was appointed director.
Three large rooms and two smaller side rooms of the palace were set aside
for the museum, which comprised paintings, drawings, sculpture, examples of
the decorative arts, and curiosa. Its principal holdings were a selection of
225 paintings from the Huis ten Bosch gallery; sixty-five paintings purchased

1

REMBRANDT VAN RIJN (1606-69)

The Company of Captain Frans Banning Cocq
or *The Night Watch*

Oil on canvas, 11' 9¹/₈" × 14' 4¹/₂"
Signed and dated lower left center:
Rembrandt f. 1642
Lent by the City of Amsterdam

This large painting is Rembrandt's most widely known masterpiece. It represents a group of Amsterdam civic guards being directed by their captain and lieutenant to form in marching order. The men advance from the shadows of a building into the sunshine of the street. Owing to discoloration of the varnish and to accumulated grime, the picture had darkened so much by the end of the eighteenth century that its meaning was no longer understood, and it was mistakenly called *The Night Watch*.

The canvas was originally commissioned for the large meeting hall of the "Kloveniers," or arquebusiers. Rembrandt painted it when he was thirty-five, at the height of his powers. By the refined distribution of light and shadow, to which all other elements are subordinated, he splendidly solved the difficult problem of bringing life and movement into a composition that had to include a great number of individual portraits.

The Night Watch Gallery

for the imposing sum of 100,000 guilders at the Van der Pot van Groeneveld
auction six weeks after the foundation of the museum; and seven important
paintings contributed by the city of Amsterdam, among them Rembrandt's
Night Watch and *The Sampling Officials of the Draper's Guild* (also known
as *The Syndics*), Bartholomeus van der Helst's *Banquet of the Civic Guard*,
and the younger Willem van de Velde's *Harbor of Amsterdam*. The same
year a further 137 paintings were acquired from the Van Heteren
collection. From the outset, the not particularly spacious chambers devoted to
the museum must have been uncomfortably crowded with exhibits.

In 1810 Louis Napoleon was forced to abdicate, and France annexed the
Netherlands. The royal gallery was then renamed Holland's Museum and put
under the administration of the city of Amsterdam. But in 1813 the country
recovered its independence, and the sixth William of Orange returned
triumphantly as sovereign prince. After the Congress of Vienna, he was placed
on the throne as King William I. Determined to rebuild his united kingdom
of Belgium and the Netherlands to its old glory, he launched a vigorous
cultural program. As part of it, his government took over the museum in
Amsterdam, calling it first 's Lands Museum, and soon afterward Rijksmuseum,
the name it has kept ever since.

Action was also soon taken on providing larger quarters for the collection.
At the suggestion of Apostool, who remained director, the building selected was
the Trippenhuis, a seventeenth-century patrician town house built by
Justus Vingboons for the Trip family in the street called Kloveniersburgwal.
For the next seventy years the museum shared this mansion with the Royal
Institute (now the Royal Academy of Arts and Sciences), also a creation
of Louis Napoleon.

As a result of purchases, gifts, and legacies, the collection grew steadily for the
first fifteen years of King William's reign. During the economic depression that
followed the Belgian revolt of 1830, however, stagnation set in, to last for
nearly half a century. The admirable beginning under Apostool, favored by his
royal patrons, makes even more disappointing the subsequent failure to
strengthen the collection. That the art market of the mid-nineteenth
century had much to offer is clearly attested by the rapid development of other
European museums during that period.

2

JOHANNES VERMEER (1632–75)

Woman in Blue Reading a Letter

Oil on canvas, 18¹/₄ × 15³/₈″
Painted about 1662–63
Van der Hoop Collection, lent by the City of Amsterdam

"A symphony in blue and gray" would be an appropriate title for this picture. It is perhaps the most poetic of Vermeer's rare works. In this masterpiece he attains miraculous equilibrium through extreme but controlled simplification. A subtle, silvery light fills the room and gives to the immobile figure the appearance of timelessness. In the silent world of Vermeer, only essential things are expressed.

Nevertheless, the Rijksmuseum gradually gained renown throughout Europe.
For this reason perhaps, from the middle of the century onward, criticism of
its entirely inadequate accommodations in the Trippenhuis became general.
Serious complaints were made about lack of space and bad lighting.
Whenever the Royal Academy met, one of the big rooms had to be cleared, and
for that it was sometimes necessary to roll or fold up large canvases.
At last, in the 1860s, plans were made for a new building, but more than ten
years were to pass before the authorities stirred into action. Even then they
engaged in prolonged debate before giving the commission to the architect
P. J. H. Cuypers. The site chosen was in the new southern quarter of the city.
Cuypers' building, which took nine years to construct, is the present
Rijksmuseum. At its opening, on July 13, 1885, Prime Minister Jan Heemskerk
stated that a decisive argument in favor of the building project had been the
danger of explosion and fire from large stores of paraffin in warehouses
near the Trippenhuis.
The massive red-brick edifice on the Stadhouderskade is familiar to everyone in
the Netherlands and to a great many people from other countries. With its
broad façade and high towers, the Rijksmuseum is still a dominant feature in
the townscape of Amsterdam, although the city has long since extended
far beyond it. Its construction and decoration, in Neo-Gothic style, was an
enormous project. The work involved in arranging the contents was no
less strenuous, for in moving from its old home to its new the collection
underwent an overwhelming expansion. The municipality of Amsterdam lent the
greater part of the paintings in its possession to the national art gallery.
Of these works, first in importance was the magnificent Van der Hoop collection,
which contained such paintings as Rembrandt's *Bridal Couple*, Vermeer's
Woman in Blue Reading a Letter, and Ruisdael's *Mill at Wijk bij Duurstede*.
With a collection twice as large as it had had in the Trippenhuis, the
Rijksmuseum found a spacious home for the nation's art treasures in the
numerous halls, galleries, and small rooms of the new building. But the
abundance of space, the ostentatious decoration, and, in particular, the
confusing arrangement of the collection met with sharp criticism both at
home and abroad. Some declared the building hopeless and ironically
suggested turning it into a bathing establishment. The poet Paul Verlaine,

in 1892, described the museum as "a big polychrome monument with turrets, the only impressive monument in Amsterdam; it is neither beautiful nor ugly, but it is undeniably big."

Later generations, however, formed a different opinion once it became apparent that, by dynamic planning, the architectural qualities of the building could be put to advantage. The modernization started laboriously after the First World War, was interrupted by the Second, and is not yet completed. Radical alterations were undertaken, with a triple aim: to make the tour of the museum logical and easy, to dispell the solemn atmosphere that depresses visitors in so many old museums, and to exhibit the collections to better advantage by means of strict selection and careful arrangement. Even today there are innumerable problems still to be solved. The collections are varied and constantly growing. How best to display them? The building is now eighty years old. How best to adapt it to modern needs? Yet despite its shortcomings, this museum has a character very much its own.

The Rijksmuseum has now become a collection of collections. In addition to the department of paintings, best known to the general public, it includes the extensive and important departments of sculpture and decorative art and of Dutch History, the Print Room, the library, and the Asian Museum. Every year this group of collections welcomes an increasing number of visitors, who come to Amsterdam from all parts of the world, drawn by *The Night Watch* and other masterpieces of Dutch art.

From the beginning the accent in the collections forming the Rijksmuseum has been placed on the art and history of the Netherlands. After the First World War, however, new departments, devoted to the painting and decorative art of other countries, were created. The policy in the Rijksmuseum has always been directed at rounding out the picture of the nation's own artistic expression. This is understandable, in view of the great prestige of seventeenth-century Dutch art. One advantage of such a restriction in program is that a single distinct line runs through the collections.

The department of paintings derives its unique character not only from the masterpieces it contains, but also from the excellent works by artists considered of the second rank. One of the astonishing phenomena of history, never yet satisfactorily explained, is that the first two generations of the seventeenth

century produced so many painters in Holland and that the general standard of
their art was so high. Even their contemporaries were conscious that something
unusual was happening, and foreign visitors noted with interest the
Dutch obsession for paintings. Observing how paintings were sold at a fair in
Rotterdam, the traveler John Evelyn wrote in his diary, in 1641: "The
reason for their store of pictures and their cheapness proceed from their want of
land, to employ their stock; so as it is an ordinary thing to find a common
farmer lay out two or three thousand pounds in this commodity; their
houses are full of them and they vend them at Kermesses to very great gains."
And another Englishman, Peter Mundy, had remarked a year before:
"All in general striving to adorn their houses, especially the outer or street
room, with costly pictures, butchers and bakers not much inferior in their
shops, which are fairly set forth, yea many times blacksmiths, cobblers etc.,
will have some picture or other by their forge and in their stalls."
Of this amazing production of paintings the Rijksmuseum shows an
uninterrupted pageant, from the fifteenth century to the late years of the
nineteenth. Inevitably there are some gaps in the survey, but not many,
and gradually they are being filled. For instance, until recently the
little-known Dutch masters of the earliest period had not received much
attention, and the museum possessed only a modest collection of their works.
Now this has changed, and, with few exceptions, the late medieval and
early Renaissance masters of the Northern Netherlands are well represented.
Some have been identified: Geertgen tot Sint Jans, Jan Mostaert, Jacob
Cornelisz. van Oostsanen, Cornelis Engebrechtsz., Lucas van Leyden,
Jan van Scorel, Maerten van Heemskerck; others are still nameless: the Master
of the Virgo inter Virgines, the Master of Alkmaar; all are important artists.
The display of the painting collection is chronological and, where possible,
grouped according to artists who worked in one center and who may therefore
have some characteristics in common. Such groups, now called schools,
are often named after the towns where the painters congregated. The Schools of
Haarlem, Delft, Leiden, Utrecht, and Amsterdam are designations as
significant and valid as the Schools of Venice and Florence.
Dutch painters, and especially those of the seventeenth century, have had a
strong tendency to specialize in subject matter. Thus Frans Hals limited himself

3

REMBRANDT VAN RIJN (1606–69)

Rembrandt's Mother

Oil on oak, 25⅝ × 18⅞″
Signed with monogram and dated lower left:
RHL 1631

Rembrandt's extraordinary spiritual growth
and technical development can be followed
clearly in his twenty paintings now in the
Rijksmuseum. Among his early works, one
of the most fascinating is the panel on
which he painted his mother absorbed in her
study of the Bible. It is not a portrait, for
the red velvet cloak and the gold-
embroidered headdress in which she poses
show that she was intended to represent
some historical or biblical figure. In the
nineteenth century she was popularly
thought to portray the prophetess Anna of
the New Testament, but this interpretation
is doubtful. Early as the painting is,
Rembrandt reveals in it his mastery of the
chiaroscuro technique—a highly personal
mastery, in which light becomes a
mysterious and precious envelope of form.

almost exclusively to group and individual portraits, which dominate the
Haarlem School. But other examples of specialization are brilliantly
represented in the Rijksmuseum: landscapes by Esaias van de Velde, Hendrick
Avercamp, Jan van Goyen, and the Ruisdaels; church interiors by Pieter
Saenredam; portraits by Jan Molenaer and Johannes Verspronck;
still lifes by Jan van de Velde and Pieter Claesz.; scenes of peasant life by
Adriaen van Ostade.

Paulus Potter devoted himself to placid scenes of rural life and farm animals;
Jan Steen, the acute observer of middle-class manners and morals, painted many
an interior full of lively individuals amusing themselves. In Amsterdam,
portrait and marine painting held the ascendancy, as shown by Bartholomeus
van der Helst's masterful portraits and the naval canvases by Willem van de
Velde the Younger. A special room is reserved for the works of the
Dutch landscape painters who journeyed to Italy and were strongly impressed
by the romantic scenery and sunny atmosphere of the Apennine hills and the
Roman Campagna.

Rembrandt ranks supreme among Dutch artists and in the Rijksmuseum
collection. Though other galleries abroad can boast a larger number of his
works, the Rijksmuseum, with its twenty paintings from the master's youth to
his old age, proudly displays the astonishing development of his genius
and treasures some of his most glorious creations. The so-called *Night Watch*,
his largest canvas and a daringly original composition, is the most widely
known. Yet the loftiness of conception and splendor of his brushwork in
The Sampling Officials of the Drapers' Guild and *The Bridal Couple* make
these works hardly less famous. Moreover, the collection contains such
outstanding works as the dramatic fragment from *The Anatomy Lesson of
Dr. Joan Deyman*, the rare sunlit landscape *The Stone Bridge*, the monumental
St. Peter's Denial, and moving portraits of the artist, his mother, and his
son Titus.

Another summit in Dutch painting is the art of the masters of pictures in small
format, called cabinet pictures. Of these the Rijksmuseum owns some of the
finest. The pearls among them are the four canvases by Johannes Vermeer
of Delft, each showing a distinct aspect of the refined and intensely
concentrated art of this rare master. The uniquely luminous quality of

4

GERARD TER BORCH (1617–81)

Helena van der Schalcke as a Child

Oil on oak, 13³/₈ × 11¹/₄"
Painted about 1644

Probably the most winsome figure in the
Rijksmuseum, sweet little Helena, a
daughter of pastor Hendrick van der
Schalcke, resembles a small bird as she steps
forward from the darkness, glancing shyly at
the painter. Ter Borch, a master of
distinguished small portraits of upper-class
people, has expressed with exceptional
sympathy the seriousness typical of
tender age.

Woman in Blue Reading a Letter, *The Kitchenmaid*, *The Little Street*, and *The Letter* pervades the room of the Delft School. But there, too, are the exquisite interiors by Pieter de Hooch and the powerful church interiors by Emanuel de Witte, and around the corner are the delicate portraits by Gerard ter Borch, who worked mainly in Deventer.

Although the Golden Age of painting ended in the Netherlands with the seventeenth century, the tradition of painting was by no means extinguished. The eighteenth century produced excellent painters of portraits, flowers, and townscapes. Chief among the portraitists was Cornelis Troost, many of whose pleasant, spirited group and individual portraits are displayed. Portrait and landscape became the customary motifs in the first part of the nineteenth century, when the painters of the Neoclassic and Romantic movements demonstrated their amazing professional skill. The Rijksmuseum has a large and representative group of paintings from the late nineteenth-century Impressionist schools of The Hague and Amsterdam, headed by the Maris brothers and George Hendrik Breitner. The main portion of this group comes from a generous bequest by Mr. and Mrs. J. C. J. Drucker-Fraser.

Because of its wealth of paintings by national masters, the Rijksmuseum has become the mecca for all lovers of Dutch art. The department of paintings also contains small collections from foreign schools, some pieces of which are exceptional. Such, for instance, are the portraits *Giuliano da Sangallo* and *Francesco Giamberti* by the Florentine Piero di Cosimo, a *Mary Magdalene* by the Venetian Carlo Crivelli, an early religious composition by Tintoretto, the striking portrait *Don Ramón Satué* by Goya, and a choice collection of delicate pastels by the eighteenth-century cosmopolitan Swiss artist, Jean-Étienne Liotard.

Though different in character from the painting collection, the department of sculpture and decorative art is no less important. The department started modestly about 1875, when it was founded as a separate Netherlands Museum for History and Art in The Hague. Soon after the completion of the new building in Amsterdam, it was incorporated in the Rijksmuseum, and from that moment dates its steady growth. Originally, interest was focused on the historic and didactic significance of the collected items; later development brought more and more to the fore the intrinsic artistic value of the sculptures

5

JEAN-ÉTIENNE LIOTARD (1702–89)

Mademoiselle Lavergne or *La Belle Liseuse*

Pastel on parchment, 21¹/₄ × 16¹/₂"
Signed and dated center right:
J. E. Liotard lion 1746

One of the finest collections of pastels by the
Swiss painter Liotard was bequeathed to
the Rijksmuseum by his Dutch descendants.
Born in Geneva and educated in Paris,
Liotard traveled widely throughout Europe
and the Levant as a fashionable pastel
portraitist. In 1756 he married Marie
Fargues, the daughter of a French merchant
living in Amsterdam, and settled with her
in Geneva.
His skill and taste are evident in the sensitive
portrait of his pretty niece. The pastel was
done in Lyons, and Mlle. Lavergne wears
the costume of a Lyons country girl. Her
lovely casual pose and delicate coloring
make her the image of feminine grace. This
portrait was so popular that Liotard made
several copies of it.

and objects of decorative art. Now the display of the collections tends to
show the heights of taste and technical skill attained by sculptors, potters,
silversmiths, glass blowers, cabinetmakers, and tapestry weavers in the
Netherlands, from the late Middle Ages till the beginning of the nineteenth
century.

The department, in fact, comprises a great variety of collections. As in the
department of paintings, the accent lies on the products of national artists and
craftsmen, but is by no means strictly limited to them. Of particular
interest are such notable examples of European decorative art as the collections
of jewelry, German and Italian rock-crystal vessels, eighteenth-century
French furniture, and Dresden china.

Nowhere, however, exists a richer survey of the plastic and decorative arts of
the Netherlands. Only the highlights can be listed here: the late Gothic wood
carvings, including refined and poignant groups and figures by Adriaen
van Wesel and the Master of Joachim and Anne; the Flemish bronze figures of
members of the House of Burgundy, from the tomb of Isabeau de Bourbon;
the rare seventeenth-century marble and terracotta sculptures by Hendrick de
Keyser, Artus Quellinus, and Rombout Verhulst. Special mention should be
made of the silver collection, which includes early guild pieces, such as
drinking horns and ceremonial chains, and some of the most lavish expressions
of the Dutch Baroque style, exemplified in the works of the Van Vianen family
and Johannes Lutma. Blue and white and polychromed pottery from Delft, one
of Europe's great ceramic centers, is splendidly represented by examples
of the various types produced in the best factories. Other showcases display
diamond-engraved green and white glass, long a Dutch speciality. The museum
also possesses a collection of Meissen porcelain second only to that at Dresden.
The furniture collection is one of the most interesting of its kind. It
stresses the evolution of the Dutch interior through successive periods of fashion
from the wealthy seventeenth century onward. Two precious dollhouses
charmingly illustrate the furnishing of the Dutch home in the Golden Age. The
tapestry section has been expanded recently by a number of rare Dutch
hangings, among which those by Frans Spiering deserve special attention.
The department of national history in the Rijksmuseum has particular
importance because it brings to life many events in the country's past by means

6

ROCHUS JACOBSZ. HOPPESTEYN
(died 1692)

Pitcher

Delft pottery, height 9⁷/₈″
Signed with the letters R.Ï.H.S. and a
Moor's head
Between 1680 and 1692

Of the Delft pottery factories in the
seventeenth century, Rochus Hoppesteyn's
Young Moor's Head was the best. He
owned it from 1680 until his death in 1692,
and proudly painted his initials on the pieces
he made himself.
This fine pitcher he painted in blue, red,
green, and gold on a clear white base. The
figures he borrowed from Chinese porcelain
patterns of the late Ming period,
interpreting them in a completely individual
style. The great difference in quality between
pieces like this and the work of other Delft
potteries is clearly shown by the details of
the garments and the handling of the
gold foliage.

7

Model by
JOHANN JOACHIM KÄNDLER
(1707–75)

Cockatoo

Meissen porcelain, height 13⁵/₈″
Dated 1734

The technique of making hard-paste
porcelain was developed in Saxony about
1708. Soon the industry began to flourish at
Meissen near Dresden, where Augustus the
Strong, Elector of Saxony, founded a factory
that successfully produced tableware and
figurines. Appointed chief modeler in 1731,
J. J. Kändler greatly stimulated the
manufacture of figures, both human and
animal, and single or in groups. His
modeling, of which this *Cockatoo* is a
spirited example, was astonishingly
vivacious. The skillful use of bright and
subdued colors on the glittering white of the
porcelain strongly reinforces the plasticity
of the model.

of authentic period relics and pictures. The struggle against Spain and
the rise of the Republic, the wars against England and France, the colonial
expansion in the East and in the West, the ventures of the Orange Stadholders—
these are some of the aspects of Dutch history illustrated not only by
paintings and engravings contemporary to the events, but also by many other
objects. There are riddled flags brought home from famous sea battles; the heraldic
decoration from the stern of the British flagship *Royal Charles*, hanging over a
collection of Admiral de Ruyter's personal belongings; the exceptional find of
tools and utensils left at Novaya Zemlya in 1596–97 by a Dutch expedition
that had almost legendary adventures; and the inscribed tin plate nailed to a
pole on the Australian west coast by skipper Dirck Hartogh's crew, possibly
the first Europeans to set foot on the island continent. Fine early ship
models and naval paintings by the Van de Veldes, father and son, are not only
valuable documents for the knowledge of shipbuilding and rigging, but also
high artistic achievements.

The treasures of the Print Room are so vast that only minor parts are familiar
to the general public. An old and constantly growing collection of prints
and drawings, it aims primarily at being the most representative repertory of the
national graphic arts. The Print Room also keeps important groups of foreign
drawings and engravings, including unique collections of early Italian and
German masters—the German Master of the Hausbuch is also called the
Master of the Amsterdam Cabinet, since it is here that most of his delicate
drypoints are found. Here also are many of Albrecht Dürer's magnificent
woodcuts and engravings. But there is hardly a Dutch graphic artist
from the fifteenth to the end of the nineteenth century not represented in the
Print Room. The splendid set of etchings by that rarest of masters, Hercules
Seghers, is world famous. The collection of a thousand Rembrandt etchings is
considered one of the best, as is the group of about one hundred drawings,
illustrating his excellence and versatility as a draftsman.

Apart from their artistic importance, the Print Room collections also have
considerable documentary significance. Countless historical portraits,
topographical drawings and charts, and prints depicting the history of the
Netherlands, added to one of the largest art libraries in Europe, constitute a
valuable center for scholarly research.

HERCULES SEGHERS
(c. 1589–c. 1638)

The Valley

Colored etching, 5⁵/₈ × 7¹/₂"

The work of this singular painter and etcher
was held in high esteem by Rembrandt,
who could justly value the older master's
powerful imagination and technical
originality. To achieve the plastic and color
effects he desired, Seghers invented new
processes of etching and printing. From any
one plate he drew prints in varying colors
and on different grades of paper. He even
made proofs on linen, strangely suggesting a
kind of printed painting.
Some of his fantastic mountain panoramas,
of which *The Valley* is one, illustrate the
wide range of atmospheric variations he
obtained by this ingenious method. His style
was vigorous, almost sculptural, expressing
the majesty of the wild landscapes and man's
minuteness in nature. Frequently he used
the motif of dead fir stumps to accentuate
a tragic mood. Little is known of
Seghers' life. He worked in Haarlem,
Amsterdam, Utrecht, and The Hague.

Up to recent times Oriental art was outside the scope of the Rijksmuseum, although the Near East was represented by a small group of ceramics and a few rugs. Thanks to important accessions after the Second World War, this section now occupies a large room. The latest and largest addition to the Rijksmuseum, however, is the entirely new Museum of Asian Art. Belonging to the Society of Friends of Asian Art, the collection has been housed since 1952 in ten rooms on the ground floor of the so-called Drucker wing. The collection covers the wide area of art from the mainland of Asia to the islands of Indonesia. Although collecting began only some four decades ago and has had to remain on a modest scale, the Museum has a number of outstanding Indian and Javanese stone and bronze sculptures, Chinese wooden statues, and later Chinese porcelain.

The Rijksmuseum has advanced a long way from the five rooms of paintings with which it began in 1808 to its present position as one of the world's leading art collections. Rich as it is, it is still moving forward, endeavoring always to improve its standards of quality. To those who know its history, it stands as a monument to the wise magistrates and liberal benefactors who established and endowed it so generously, for the enlightenment and enjoyment of mankind.

A. F. E. van Schendel

Room from a House in Haarlem

About 1790

This room from the house of Willem Ph. Kops in Haarlem is complete in every detail: the silk wall-covering from France, the carpet, the curtains, the crystal candelabra on the mantelpiece, the furniture upholstered in brocaded silk damask. The colors of the woodwork—blue-gray, light green, and white—were inspired by the palette of Josiah Wedgwood, the great English potter. Beautifully ornamented with sculptured allegorical figures, acanthus tendrils, and flower garlands, the woodwork was probably made from a design by the Amsterdam architect Abraham van der Hart (1747–1820). This eighteenth-century room is one of the few preserved entirely in its original condition.

Some of the Galleries of the Rijksmuseum

Gallery of Honor: Paintings by Non-Dutch Masters

Painting Gallery: Early Seventeenth-Century Dutch School

Sculpture Gallery

Sculpture Gallery

Gallery with Altar from Church at Rijsbergen, and Dutch Seventeenth-Century Engraved Glass and Silver

Dutch Porcelain Gallery, with View of Dutch Empire Gallery

Dutch Louis XVI Room

Paintings

GEERTGEN TOT SINT JANS
(c. 1460–c. 1495)

The Holy Kinship

Oil on oak, 54¹/₈ × 41³/₈"

Geertgen is considered the most personal of
the early Dutch painters. Presumably born
in Leiden, he worked in Haarlem, where
he was the pupil of Albert van Ouwater
and later lived with the Brotherhood
of St. John. (The name Geertgen tot Sint
Jans means the little Gerrit who lives with
the St. John Brothers.) He died young, and
few of his paintings are extant.
Almost a family group portrait, *The Holy
Kinship* depicts Christ's immediate relatives
gathered in the interior of a Gothic church.
To the left sits Anne, mother of the
Virgin, and next to her Mary with Jesus on
her lap. Behind them stand their
husbands, Joachim with a staff and Joseph
with a flowering lily branch. Young
James the Less, holding his fuller's club, is in
front of Joachim. At the far right Elisabeth
sits with the small John the Baptist, who
stretches out his arms to the Christ Child.
Behind Elisabeth are Mary Salome and
Mary Cleophas, who has an open book
on her knees. Their husbands, Zacharias,
Zebedee, and Alpheus, stand facing forward
beside the altar. In the middle of the
colorful tile floor are three little boys playing
with their holy emblems: Simon Zelotes
with the saw, John the Evangelist with the
chalice, and James the Greater with a
pilgrim's flask, from which he is pouring
wine. Judas Thaddeus lights a candle on the
choir screen.
With its lively colors and rich details, the
painting delights the eye. The holiness of
the figures portrayed is suggested not
by means of the customary halos, but by
their expressions of serenity and earnest
humility.

GEERTGEN TOT SINT JANS
(c. 1460–c. 1495)

The Tree of Jesse

Oil on oak, 35 × 23¹/₄″

Like the theme of the Holy Kinship, that of
the Jesse Tree afforded artists an opportunity
to depict Christ's forebears. The motif
appeared frequently in medieval prints and
paintings. For the most part, these
representations were purely decorative,
the branches and leaves of the tree
being treated as ornaments. Geertgen's Jesse
Tree is an exception: it is a real tree in
realistic surroundings.

Jesse lies sleeping in a little garden enclosed
by a low wall within the courtyard of a
cloister, the arches of which are just visible
through the foliage. Out of him sprouts
the tree which bears the kings of Judah.
At the bottom is David with his harp, and
next to him, precariously balanced on
the lowest branch, is Solomon. The other
nobles cannot be identified with certainty.
To the left and right of Jesse stand Isaiah
and Jeremiah, who prophesy that Jesus
will spring from David's line. The nun in
white habit kneeling in the left foreground is
the donatress of the painting.

The wonderful blend of realism and fantasy,
the rich colors of the kings' costumes,
and the purity of the details make *The Tree
of Jesse* one of the most beautiful panels
painted in Holland in the late Middle
Ages. It is also sometimes ascribed to
Geertgen's pupil, Jan Mostaert.

MASTER OF ALKMAAR
(active first half of sixteenth century)

The Seven Acts of Charity

Oil on oak, outer panels 39³/₄ × 21¹/₄″,
inner 39³/₄ × 21⁷/₈″
Dated on the original frame: 1504

This series of seven panels enclosed in o
frame depicts the six acts of charity
described in the Gospel of St. Matthew:
feeding the hungry, refreshing the thirsty
ing the naked, sheltering pilgrims,
sick, and comforting captive
welfth century a seventh
the traditional six-
wn here in

th

to
n a

ortant
urch of
lled the
e Master of
rked only
owever, and ha

13 and 13a

JAN MOSTAERT (c. 1475–c. 1555)

Portrait of a Lady

Oil on oak, 25¹/₄ × 19¹/₂"
Painted about 1520–25

Springing from the late-medieval tradition in
Haarlem, Mostaert worked there and also
in the Southern Netherlands at the Malines
court of Margaret of Austria. He excelled in
portrait and landscape, which were later to
become the specialities of Dutch painters.
The two motifs are happily combined
in this portrait full of light and space.
The Miracle of St. Hubert, patron of
hunters, which is depicted in the background,
seems to be an allusion to the nobility
of the sitter, who is dressed in a brown,
fur-trimmed robe with red undersleeves.

14, 14a, and 14b

LUCAS VAN LEYDEN (c. 1489–1533)

Triptych: The Adoration of the Golden Calf

Oil on oak, central panel 36⁵/₈ × 26³/₈",
wings 35⁷/₈ × 11³/₄"
Late work

One of the most gifted Dutch artists of his
time, Lucas van Leyden died young.
His paintings, engravings, and drawings
show his extraordinary draftsmanship.
Although influenced by Albrecht Dürer,
whom he met in Antwerp, and by his
Flemish contemporaries, he elaborated a
personal Renaissance style.
This story of Moses, an unusual subject for
a triptych, allowed him to display a
surprising variety of movements and
attitudes. An excited rhythm pervades the
reveling crowds, while in the distance,
under a dark cloud, Moses descends from
Mount Sinai with the stone tables of the Law.

JAN VAN SCOREL (1495–1562)

Mary Magdalene

Oil on oak, 26³/₈ × 30¹/₈"
Probably painted about 1527–29

Jan van Scorel was born in Schoorl, a
village on the North Holland coast. He
attended the Latin School in nearby
Alkmaar and remained in that town for his
first training as a painter under Cornelis
Buys. Later he studied with Jacob
Cornelisz. van Oostsanen in Amsterdam.
Before he set out on his great pilgrimage to
the Holy Land, in 1519, he also worked
for a short time in the studio of Jan
Gossaert, called Mabuse, in Utrecht.
Upon his return from Palestine, Scorel
lingered in Italy, especially in Venice and
Rome. For two years he served as
custodian of the Vatican art treasures, a
position Raphael had occupied shortly
before. These Italian experiences were of
decisive influence on Jan van Scorel's style
for the rest of his life. In the autumn of 1524
he returned to the Netherlands, thereafter
working mainly in Utrecht.
His *Mary Magdalene*, for which his wife,
Agatha van Schoonhoven, served as model,
is reminiscent of Venetian beauties as
Giorgione or Palma saw them. The exotic
landscape stirs memories of the
fantastic mountain formations and valleys
of the Dolomites. Even the colors have
an ardor more Venetian than Dutch.

MAERTEN VAN HEEMSKERCK
(1498–1574)

Pieter Bicker Gerritsz. and *Anna Codde*

Oil on oak, each panel 33¹/₄ × 25⁵/₈″
Dated on original frames: 1529. A. 34
and 1529. A. 26

From an early stage Dutch portraitists tended to render the appearance of their models with sober realism, feeling no inclination to flatter and idealize. Sometimes the setting helped to emphasize the true-to-nature likeness of the sitter, as in these portraits of well-to-do Amsterdam burghers. Bicker, who was master of the mint, looks up from his accounting work. His wife remains sweetly and calmly occupied with her spinning wheel, at that time a relatively new invention with high social standing. The modeling is precise and powerful. These decorative portraits are tentatively attributed to the young Heemskerck, who was a pupil of Jan van Scorel in Haarlem, where he worked all his life except for a visit to Italy from 1532 to 1535.

ANTHONIS MOR VAN DASHORST
(1519–75)

Sir Thomas Gresham

Oil on oak, 35³/₈ × 29³/₄"
Painted about 1560

Cool distinction marks the portraits which Anthonis Mor painted at many courts of Europe. The commissions from his royal or aristocratic patrons took the celebrated Dutch portraitist to Italy, Spain, and Portugal (where he was called Antonio Moro), and to England (where he may or may not have been knighted by Queen Mary for painting her portrait, but at least was known as Sir Anthony More). Apart from his travels, he worked mainly in Utrecht, where he was born, and Antwerp, where he died.

The portraits of Sir Thomas Gresham and his wife (also in the Rijksmuseum) were probably painted in Antwerp. Sir Thomas, Queen Elizabeth's financial agent in the Netherlands, had his headquarters there. He later returned to London, where he founded the Royal Exchange and, by provisions of his will, Gresham College. With wonderful psychological penetration the painter has fixed the keenly observant eye of his sitter.

JACOB CORNELISZ.
VAN OOSTSANEN (c. 1470–1533)

Self-Portrait

Oil on oak, 15 × 11³/₄″
Signed with initials and dated at left:
I A 1533

Jacob Cornelisz. van Oostsanen is also
called Jacob Cornelisz. van Amsterdam.
Oostsanen refers to his birthplace, Oostzaan,
near Zaandam; Amsterdam, to the city
where he worked. He was one of the first
great painters of Amsterdam, a small but
growing municipality at the beginning of the
sixteenth century. As its economy
flourished, so did its art and science.
Humanism gained ground, and the first
harbingers of the Renaissance began to
penetrate the Northern Netherlands.
Jacob's *Self-Portrait*, created in the year he
died, is a clear expression of the new
intellectual ferment. It is the earliest
independent self-portrait in the
Rijksmuseum's collection. On a little piece
of paper pinned with a stroke of the
brush to the background, the artist placed
his initials, *I A*, with his house-mark
between them, and the date 1533.

CORNELIS CORNELISZ.
VAN HAERLEM (1562–1638)

Bathsheba

Oil on canvas, 30¹/₂ × 25¹/₄″
Signed with monogram and dated lower left:
1594

Cornelis Cornelisz. was a member of an
academy established by a few artists
in Haarlem shortly before 1583. These
artists, and another group in Utrecht,
introduced Italian and French Mannerism
into the Netherlands. Cornelis Cornelisz. was
one of the most important representatives
of the new style, which found little response
and was soon superseded. For the most part
he painted large canvases with biblical
or mythological subjects and many nude
figures. His small paintings, of which this
poetic *Bathsheba* is one, show his delicate
sense of form and color far better than do
his crowded large compositions.

21

JAN BRUEGHEL THE ELDER
(1568–1625)

Flower Piece

Oil on copper, 9⁵/₈ × 7¹/₂″

Jan Brueghel was the son of Pieter Brueghel
the Elder ("Peasant" Brueghel). Unlike his
brother, Pieter Brueghel the Younger
("Hell" Brueghel), Jan was in no way a
slavish imitator of his famous father, but
developed a wholly individual style.
His landscapes, mostly small in size, are of
an amazing delicacy and gained him the
nickname "Velvet" Brueghel. His work was
often imitated, and until well into the
eighteenth century some artists continued to
paint in his style. This little flower piece,
of narcissi, columbine, a carnation, and
garlic in a goblet, bears witness to his good
taste and great technical style.

22 and 22a

JOOS DE MOMPER (1564–1635)

Riverside Landscape with a Boar Hunt

Oil on oak, 47⁵/₈ × 77³/₈"

The landscape painter of the sixteenth
century never attempted to give a true
picture of reality. His dream-wrought
landscapes, often depicting one of the
months or seasons, were constructed of
disparate elements borrowed from nature.
This broad landscape by Joos de Momper of
Antwerp is thus typically composed from
studies he had made in nature. Between
1581 and 1590 he traveled in Italy and
Switzerland, and he seems to have lived for
the rest of his life on the impressions he
accumulated there. His paintings seldom
lack fantastic rock formations or
waterfalls, unlike anything he could have
seen in the vicinity of his birthplace.
In this *Riverside Landscape*, the hunting
party in the left foreground attracts only
passing attention. Rather, the spectator is
drawn to the heavy rock masses, left
and right, crowned with strange
Renaissance structures, and especially to the
entrancing vista of the endless river valley
with its towns and fleets of ships.

PIETER PIETERSZ.
(c. 1543–1603)

Man and Woman with Spinning Wheel

Oil on oak, 29⅞ × 24¾"
Signed with a P and a trident
Painted about 1575–80

The symbolism of sixteenth- and seventeenth-
century paintings is often unclear today.
That this domestic scene had a particular
meaning is very probable. The woman has
been spinning and is now winding the wool
from the reel onto the spool. The man
behind her holds a pewter pitcher. In a few
contemporaneous paintings, similar
compositions portray the libertine life of the
Prodigal Son. This picture may well
represent amorous dalliance, but the
woman's modesty excludes the possibility
that the man is the Prodigal Son.
The painting makes a festive impression.
The man is clad in an ocher yellow doublet,
red breeches, and black hat, the woman in a
black bodice with yellowish-green
undersleeves, and a red and yellow skirt
showing beneath her white apron. Pieter
Pietersz. often cropped his compositions,
as he does here, giving his works their own
intimacy and charm.

ABRAHAM BLOEMAERT
(1564–1651)

The Preaching of John the Baptist

Oil on canvas, 54³/₄ × 74″
Signed below, right center: A. Blommaert
Painted about 1600

In a mountainous landscape John the
Baptist stands in the shadow of a massive
tree. Around him are gathered men and
women, some listening, others sleeping; in
the foreground, a mother feeds her child.
The trunks and branches of the trees
and the play of lines of the mountains form
a restless pattern, to which the attitudes
of the foreground figures wholly correspond,
so that the painting is pervaded with
motion.

Bloemaert belongs among the painters
at the end of the sixteenth century who
attached themselves to Mannerism, a style
that flourished particularly in such
great European centers as Vienna, Prague,
and Paris. This style also attracted many
followers in Haarlem and in Utrecht,
where Bloemaert worked. Perhaps the best
and most original representative of the
Utrecht group, he was a versatile artist who
was famous in his time and had many pupils.

SALOMON MESDACH
(active first half of seventeenth century)

Anna Boudaen Courten

Oil on oak, 37³/₄ × 27¹/₂″
Dated right background: A° 1619

Of the countless portrait painters who
worked in the Netherlands in the seventeenth
century, the Middelburg artist Salomon
Mesdach is one of the least known. Yet this
portrait of Anna Boudaen Courten
(1599–1621), member of a prominent
Zeeland family, outcharms many others
from the beginning of the century. Anna
and her husband, Jacob Pergens,
commissioned companion portraits in 1619,
the year of their marriage, and Mesdach
captured with rare excellence the young
bride in all her feminine grace and
fashionable clothes.

26

DAVID VINCKBOONS
(1576–c.1632)

The Garden Party

Oil on oak, 11¹/₄ × 17¹/₄″
Painted soon after 1610

The first half of the Eighty Years' War was
fought in the latter part of the sixteenth
century. After long and fierce struggles, the
Protestant Northern Netherlands
separated from the Catholic South, and
many Protestant Flemish artists made their
way to the Dutch provinces. Among these
emigrants was a group of painters
who reinvigorated the treatment of
landscape in the centers where they settled.
One of them was Vinckboons, whose gay,
romantic *Garden Party* strikes a fresh
note in the restrained art of the sober North.
His ladies and their gallants revel the
hours away in Cupid's abode, the rich
colors of their costumes contrasting vividly
with the shadowy green of the park.

27 and 27a

ADRIAEN PIETERSZ.
VAN DE VENNE
(1589–1662)

The Harbor at Middelburg

Oil on oak, 25¹/₄ × 53"
Painted between 1613 and 1625

On May 7, 1613, the Count Palatine
Frederick V and his wife arrived from
England to visit Frederick's uncle, Prince
Maurice of Orange-Nassau, at Middelburg
in Zeeland. On May 12 the countess
continued her journey, and it is
presumably the scene of her departure that
Van de Venne depicted. The artist then lived
in Middelburg and is thought to have
included himself in his painting, as the third
horseman in the water at the foot of the
dike (see detail).
Adriaen van de Venne was primarily an
illustrator. His brother, Jan Pietersz. van de
Venne, was an art dealer and publisher,
and many beautiful books issued by his
house were illustrated by Adriaen. A first-
rate figure painter, Adriaen was also
greatly skilled in depicting the countless
details of daily life. Moreover, he
understood the construction and rigging of
ships. Effortlessly combining these qualities,
he filled this harbor panel with hundreds of
details, all accurate, all painted with care.
Adriaen himself once said, "Painting
gives me great joy," and something of this
joy is communicated across the centuries
by this lively farewell procession.

28, 28a, and 28b

HENDRICK AVERCAMP (1585–1634)

Large Winter Scene

Oil on oak, 30¹/₂ × 52″
Signed at right, on wall of shed: Henricus Av

For centuries the Dutch have flocked to the
ice in winter, but few paintings capture
the national pastime so fully and accurately
as does this large panel. The painter
looks down, as if from a tower, upon the
wintry village. Snow has fallen, covering the
fields and rooftops; trees and birds are
starkly silhouetted against the leaden sky.
The broad, frozen water is teeming
with people. The master skaters glide
gracefully by, singly or in pairs. Others, less
skillful, struggle to keep upright or fall
prostrate on the ice. In the center
foreground, a game of *kolf*—the forerunner
of both ice hockey and golf—is in progress.
A child on a sled is pushed gaily along,
and other sleds, pulled by beautifully
harnessed horses, move about on the ice.
A beggar humbly approaches a group
of prosperous citizens who stand talking
together.
Avercamp, called the Mute of Kampen,
was deaf and dumb. Yet in this painting he
speaks an eternal language. With eloquent
gestures he points out the vastness of the
Dutch polder landscape, and then,
winking, he motions silently to the little
things that are happening in the hidden
corners between the farmhouses.

Large Winter Scene. Details

JOHANNES TORRENTIUS
(1589–1644)

Still Life, Allegory on Temperance

Oil on oak, oval panel, 20^1/$_2$ × 19^7/$_8$"
Signed and dated on bridle: T 1614

Johannes Torrentius' real name was
Jan Simonsz. van der Beeck. He was an
exotic figure—an outspoken Rosicrucian
and libertine, often in conflict with the law.
In 1628, after having been tortured, he
was sentenced to twenty years'
imprisonment for forgery. On the inter-
cession of King Charles I of England, to
whom this *Still Life* had been presented,
the Stadholder Frederick Henry signed his
pardon in 1630.
This panel is the only work of Torrentius
still known to exist. In painting it he
probably made use of a camera obscura.
The inscription on the sheet of music
may be translated: "*E.R.*†: *Eques Rosae
Crusis* [Rosicrucian Knight]. Whatever
exists without moderation / Perishes in
evil immoderate."

30

WILLEM BUYTEWECH
(c. 1591–1624)

County Courtships

Oil on canvas, 22 × 27^1/$_2$"
Painted about 1616–17

"Witty Willem" was the nickname of this
Rotterdam artist, who worked also in
Haarlem. His originality and inventiveness
are shown not only in his paintings, but
also in his drawings and etchings. The
subject of this attractive and colorful
painting remains a mystery, although the
elegant couples depicted seem to be engaged
in amorous conversation, perhaps about
a choice of rosebuds. Some authorities have
suggested that *County Courtships* may
celebrate the engagement of two sisters of
the Van Duvelandt van Rhoon family.

ESAIAS VAN DE VELDE (1591–1630)

The Ferry Boat

Oil on canvas, 29³/₄ × 44¹/₂″
Signed and dated right, on the fence:
E. V. Velde 1622

A river cuts through a village. Among the
trees along the banks stand simple houses
and farms, a windmill, a church. The
villagers walk about, talk, and work. A
large rectangular ferry has just embarked
from the left shore with a horse and buggy,
two cows, and several people. The
bird-filled sky is cloudy, and the placid
water reflects the peaceful scene. There is not
much more to say about this picture.
In quiet corners of Holland today it is not
difficult to find similar spots and similar
activities.
The painting's everyday reality is indeed
the greatest artistic achievement of its
creator, for artists in 1622 were seemingly
unaware of the beauty of the Dutch
landscape and practically never painted it.
In the middle of the century an Italian
contemporary wrote, "It is too bad. The
Dutch can paint very well, but they do not
know what is beautiful." The greatness of
Dutch paintings, however, lies primarily
in the artists' ability to see beauty in the
things of their daily surroundings. Esaias
van de Velde was among the first to apply
this vision to landscape, and he is therefore
justifiably called the founder of Dutch
landscape art.

JAN VAN GOYEN (1596–1656)

Summer and *Winter*

Oil on two round oak panels, diameter 13¹/₄″
Both signed and dated: I V Goien 1625

The landscape painters of the sixteenth
century took over the custom of painting
the seasons from the illuminated Books
of Hours of the Middle Ages. Although no
longer so vigorous, this tradition was
maintained even in the seventeenth century.
Whether Van Goyen created panels
depicting Spring and Autumn to
accompany these of Summer and Winter is
not known.
Jan van Goyen was one of the best landscape
painters of the seventeenth century. In
his work a clear evolution is evident, and
his undated paintings—he nearly always
signed them—can rather easily be placed
chronologically within his work. Of his
many teachers, Esaias van de Velde is the
only one whose influence can be traced
readily in Van Goyen's early work. These
two panels, with their somewhat hard
colors and the important place assigned the
figures, belong to his earliest period and
without doubt were painted under
Esaias' tutelage.

FRANS HALS (c. 1580–1666)

Isaac Massa and Beatrix van der Laen

Oil on canvas, $55^1/_8 \times 65^1/_2''$
Painted about 1622

The couple is portrayed full length, sitting under a tree in a park. The design of the painting is more thoroughly worked out than in most of Frans Hals's portraits. Only a few large canvases are known in which he depicted a family group out of doors. With masterful skill the painter has caught his subjects' relaxed air and the evanescence of their smiles. The fresh green of the foliage blends with the clear light, giving the painting an atmosphere of blithe happiness.
The portraits were formerly considered to be those of Frans Hals and his wife or of his younger brother Dirck Hals and his wife. They are now presumed to portray Isaac Massa (1586–1643), cartographer, merchant, and diplomat, and his wife Beatrix van der Laen, daughter of the burgomaster of Haarlem. The painting was perhaps created in honor of their marriage on April 25, 1622. A wedding theme is indicated by the ivy twining about the tree—long an emblem of love, marriage, and connubial faith—and by the thistle at the man's side and the ivy tendril at the woman's, analogous symbols of fidelity and conjugal love.

FRANS HALS (c. 1580–1666)

Nicolaes Hasselaer

Oil on canvas, 31¹/₄ × 26¹/₈"
Painted between 1630 and 1635

At the beginning of the seventeenth century Haarlem was one of the most flourishing artistic centers in the Netherlands. Frans Hals's parents, fleeing the Spanish terror in Antwerp, where Frans was born, settled in the North Holland town sometime after 1586; their son Dirck was born there in 1591.

Little is known of the artist's early training and development. As a boy he studied under Karel van Mander, a Flemish Mannerist painter also resident in Haarlem, and he soon began to specialize in portraits, receiving many public and private commissions. Hals's striking personal style, a blend of unconventional composition and brilliant technique, brings his sitters to life. Painted with the utmost economy, his portrait of Nicolaes Hasselaer (1593–1635), a captain-major of the Amsterdam militia, has a modern directness of expression.

FRANS HALS (c. 1580–1666)

The Jolly Toper

Oil on canvas, 31⁷/₈ × 26¹/₄"
Painted about 1628–30; signed with monogram
in right background

Hals does not conceal his handwriting; on
the contrary, he loves to show the boldness
of his brush strokes. It is fascinating to
observe how he models a face, a hand, a
glass, by a rapid juxtaposition of hatches
and dashes, not unlike the method of later
French Impressionists. From this pictorial
procedure his works derive their special
vibrant quality.

This merry drinker, as the painting is also
sometimes called, perhaps represents the
sense of taste—or the sheer joy of
drinking. The medallion in his belt may
portray Prince Maurice of Orange
(1567–1625), son of William the Silent and
himself a warrior Stadholder.

HANS BOLLONGIER or BOULENGER (c. 1600–1645)

Flowers in a Vase

Oil on oak, 26³/₄ × 21¹/₂"
Signed and dated lower right: H Boulenger 1639

As is well known, the seventeenth-century Dutch possessed a heightened fancy for flowers. They took to the recently introduced tulip with alacrity and avarice, piously cultivating rare varieties and selling them at high prices. Many painters, like the Haarlemer Bollongier, excelled in flower portraits. They usually did not paint directly from nature, but with the help of preliminary watercolor studies, which were kept as models in the studio. Despite the painstaking precision with which they reproduced forms and shades, such artists as Bollongier always achieved a pleasant decorative effect with their floral arrangements.

ADRIAEN VAN OSTADE
(1610–85)

Landscape with Oak

Oil on oak, 13¹/₄ × 18³/₄″
Painted about 1640

Although Adriaen van Ostade, a prolific
painter, concentrated almost exclusively on
peasant scenes in or around inns and
farms, he also painted a few landscapes, five
of which are known still to exist. Judging
from its style, this monochromic painting
was created about 1640 and thus belongs to
Ostade's relatively early work. At that
time his palette was limited; later he used
clear colors freely and with great refinement.
The strong light contrasts in *Landscape
with Oak* are reminiscent of Rembrandt, but
Rembrandt probably did not influence
Ostade directly in this painting. More likely
the Haarlem artist had looked at
landscapes by his popular fellow townsman
Pieter de Molijn, who often used motifs
from the dunes along the Dutch coast.

39

JAN MIENSE MOLENAER
(c. 1610–68)

A Lady at the Harpsichord

Oil on oak, 15¹/₈ × 11⁵/₈″
Painted about 1635–40

The taste of the Dutch in the Golden Age
was for portraits—portraits of people,
things, animals, ships, family life. The new
burgher generations appreciated such
finely painted interior scenes as this one,
which makes no claim to profundity but
does convey directly and clearly the popular
sense of well-being. Molenaer was a pupil of
Frans Hals and was influenced by
Adriaen Brouwer. In 1636 he married
Judith Leyster, also a pupil of Hals and
perhaps the model for this genteel
harpsichordist.

40

PIETER CLAESZ. (c. 1597–1660)

Still Life

Oil on oak, 25¹/₄ × 32¹/₄"
Signed with monogram and dated lower right:
A° 1647

Most Dutch artists in the seventeenth century were highly specialized in subject matter. Some landscape painters confined themselves to winter scenes, others to rivers, forests, or meadows. There were painters of towns and of churches, of portraits and of peasant life. The humble objects of every day were the theme of still-life painters like Pieter Claesz., who worked in Haarlem. With wonderful penetration and intensity he painted the varying reflections of silvery light on the surface of glass, pewter vessels, and foodstuffs on the corner of a table.

41

JAN VAN GOYEN (1596–1656)

Landscape with Two Oaks

Oil on canvas, 34⁷/₈ × 43¹/₂"
Signed and dated: VG 1641

After his early work (see plates 32 and 33), which was strongly influenced by Esaias van de Velde, Van Goyen developed more and more as a painter of landscapes. He introduced figures primarily to give depth to his pictures, but it was the larger scene that interested him. Originally rather varied, his colors gradually became more subdued, until at last he painted almost entirely in grays and browns, shading to greens and blues. Such a color scheme accords with the prevailing atmosphere of the low-lying Netherlands, where the misty air dulls and vitiates bright colors. This canvas, portraying two old oak trees ravished by the weather, dates from the artist's middle period, during which he still used touches of red and yellow. But the light brushing the foreground and the trees' scanty foliage is filtered and at any moment will be blotted out by the lowering rain clouds.

JOHANNES CORNELISZ.
VERSPRONCK (1597–1662)

Portrait of a Girl in Blue

Oil on canvas, $32^1/_4 \times 26^1/_8{}''$
Signed and dated lower left:
J verspronck an° 1641

Johannes Verspronck ranks next to his
teacher Frans Hals as the outstanding
portrait painter of the Haarlem School.
He has nothing of his master's vivacity, but
by patiently and intently observing his
sitters he attained a rare quality of calm
perfection. This child, fashionably dressed
in the style of a lady, a wistful smile about
to break upon her lips, has endless appeal.
Verspronck painted her with great
sensitivity and tenderness. Against the
neutral background, the pale blue shades of
her dress acquire admirable luminosity.

PIETER JANSZ. SAENREDAM
(1597–1665)

Interior of St. Odolph's Church at Assendelft

Oil on oak, 19³/₄ × 29⁷/₈″
Dated 1649
Van der Hoop Collection, lent by the City
of Amsterdam

"This is the church at Assendelft, a village in Holland, by Pieter Saenredam, this was painted in the year 1649 on 2 October" —so the painter signed this panel, on a pew at the left. Similarly explicit and complete inscriptions rarely appear on work by other painters, but are characteristic of Saenredam. His portraits of churches, which occupied him from 1628 until his death, are architecturally exact and pictorially brilliant.

Saenredam followed a fixed routine. Without using a ruler, he made a working sketch on the spot. Often he worked out difficult details separately. He nearly always signed and dated his drawings. Years might go by before he returned to his first sketches. Then, before he began painting, he made a construction drawing, transferred its lines to the panel, and at last took up his brush. He made the St. Odolph's sketch on July 31, 1634, the construction drawing on December 9, 1643, and finished the painting—as the inscription shows—on October 2, 1649, thus taking more than fifteen years to complete the project.

Time-consuming though his preparations were, once Saenredam began to paint, following the lines of his carefully worked-out pattern, he was able to express himself fully. From his hand flowed the whitewashed walls, the stone floors, the finely gleaming copper chandeliers. His paintings have a tender purity, suffused with radiant light.

He was not strong as a figure painter, but needed figures to convey the suggestion of space. Someone else, therefore, usually painted the people who thinly populate his churches. In this panel it was probably his fellow townsman of Haarlem, Adriaen van Ostade. The tombstone in the foreground is that of Saenredam's father.

JAN JANSZ. VAN DE VELDE
(1619/20–after 1663?)

Still Life

Oil on oak, 25¹/₄ × 23¹/₄″
Signed and dated on the table:
Jan van de Velde 1647

Jan Jansz. van de Velde was the son of the
draftsman and engraver Jan van de Velde.
He worked primarily in Haarlem, where
still-life painting had early developed and
flourished to great heights in the work
of Pieter Claesz. and Willem Claesz. Heda.
Without doubt these slightly older
contemporaries were looked to as models by
Jan Jansz., but he developed his own style,
even though his subject matter was limited.
The dark backgrounds he preferred
enabled him to depict objects sparkling
with light, yet like precious jewels
surrounded by an aura of mystery.

THOMAS DE KEYSER
(1596/97–1667)

Pieter Schout on Horseback

Oil on copper, 33⁷/₈ × 27³/₈"
*Signed with monogram and dated on the
saddle: 1660*

The monumental equestrian portrait never
became a popular subject in the Northern
Netherlands, mainly because most of the
people who commissioned portraits
were wealthy city dwellers. The court and
the nobility played only a small role on
the seventeenth-century artistic scene.
This mounted portrait of Pieter Schout
(1640–69), high bailiff of Hagestein, can
hardly be compared with the life-size
equestrian portraits by Rubens and
Van Dyke. It is, as it were, a Dutch
interpretation of such portraits: small in size
and minutely detailed.
Thomas de Keyser, son of the architect and
sculptor Hendrick de Keyser, was one of
the best portrait painters of Amsterdam.
The landscape in the background of this
painting has been attributed to Adriaen van
de Velde. Portraitists and landscape artists
very often collaborated on works such as this.

HENDRICK TER BRUGGHEN
(1588–1629)

The Incredulity of Thomas

Oil on canvas, 42⁷/₈ × 53³/₄"
Painted after 1614

During the sixteenth and seventeenth centuries foreign currents and influences found fertile soil in Utrecht, then an artistic center. Abraham Bloemaert (see plate 24) was the Dutch representative of Mannerism there, and his pupil Hendrick ter Brugghen, after a decade in Italy, introduced the style of Caravaggio into the sober north. In this painting Ter Brugghen depicts the disciple Thomas, who refused to believe in the resurrection of Christ, as he lays his finger in the wound in Jesus' side. The heads and hands of the figures are carefully worked out, in striking contrast to the large areas of their colorful robes. The lined and wrinkled faces catch the strong light, creating an overrealistic effect. Since the figures almost completely cover the whole surface, the canvas has a monumentality that derives directly from Italian art and was virtually unknown in native Dutch painting.

STUDIO OF REMBRANDT

Still Life with Books

Oil on oak, 35³/₄ × 47¹/₄"
Painted about 1630

Research has revealed that this large still
life was painted by two artists. The original
painting was a Vanitas, with books,
scientific instruments, and objects
symbolizing the arts. The pewter jug, the
glass, and the plate with the bread were
added later, but certainly still within the
seventeenth century. At that time it was not
unusual for "other hands" to add to
paintings.
The Vanitas is exceptionally powerful and
spirited. It has an air of the university town
Leiden about it, and Rembrandt was a
son of Leiden until he went to Amsterdam
in 1631. In fact, no one but Rembrandt
was capable of painting a still life like this.
But there is no external evidence, and
therefore no certainty, that he did. The still
life in the foreground may have been
painted by Jan Jansz. den Uyl, who is
known to have been acquainted with
Rembrandt.

48

REMBRANDT VAN RIJN
(1606–69)

The Stone Bridge

Oil on oak, 11⁵/₈ × 16³/₄"
Painted about 1638

In the few landscapes that Rembrandt
painted, he never tried to give an impression
of a real situation. Rather, these paintings
might be described as nature dramatized.
Such is this powerful little view on the
banks of a stream. The cottages amid the
trees, the bridge, the boat with fishermen,
the distant church spire—all these elements
participate in the dramatic struggle
between the sun and the threatening storm
clouds.

REMBRANDT VAN RIJN
(1606–69)

Jeremiah Lamenting the Destruction of Jerusalem

Oil on oak, 22⁷/₈ × 18¹/₈"
Signed with monogram and dated, lower right:
1630

In his youth Rembrandt painted, with few
exceptions, on wood panels of small size.
Only after his arrival in Amsterdam,
where his first big commission was *The
Anatomy Lesson of Professor Tulp*, did
he begin using canvases of larger size.
The figure Rembrandt depicts in this small
panel is presumably the prophet Jeremiah,
who has retired into solitude while
Jerusalem, ravaged by war, goes up in
flames. The dramatic content of the story
and the prophet's inner turmoil are
presented with a masterly hand. Where too
much detail would be disturbing, the
artist merely suggests, in thin paint, those
things that form the background, literally
and figuratively, of the prophet's state of
mind. The old man who served as model
appears frequently in Rembrandt's paintings
and graphic work during this period.
Nowhere is he treated with greater
solicitude.

REMBRANDT VAN RIJN
(1606–69)

The Company of Captain Frans Banning Cocq
or *The Night Watch*

Painted 1642
Details

The great merit of Rembrandt's *Night
Watch* becomes clear only when one
compares this work with other civic-guard
pieces painted at the same time. Artists
considered a commission for a full-length
group portrait perhaps the most difficult
yet the most complimentary they could
receive. They attempted in various ways to
enliven the many heads they had to deal
with, but all too often their efforts ended in
a row of monotonous faces.

Rembrandt broke completely with every
tradition. By a wholly unconstrained and
lively arrangement of figures, and especially
by a daring play of strong areas of light
and dark, he was able to surmount the
dullness of the group portrait. His clear
yellows and reds glow remarkably against
the browns and blacks of the shadows
behind them.

It is not true that the painting was
unappreciated by Rembrandt's
contemporaries. In 1678 his pupil Samuel
van Hoogstraten wrote—albeit he mingled
his praise with criticism—that the work was
so picturesque of concept, so dashing, and
so powerful that all other pieces hanging in
the same room were like so many playing
cards.

Rembrandt probably got the commission
for *The Night Watch* as a result of the
state visit paid to Amsterdam in 1638 by the
Queen of France, Marie de Médici.
Banning Cocq's company served as honor
guard to the royal guest.

REMBRANDT VAN RIJN
(1606–69)

Self-Portrait as the Apostle Paul

Oil on canvas, 35⁷/₈ × 30¹/₄″
Signed and dated left, above the shoulder:
Rembrandt. f. 1661

Rembrandt's numerous self-portraits make a
unique and moving biography of the artist.
Here he shows himself, at the age of
fifty-five, with a sword and a book, the
attributes of the apostle Paul. His recent
financial misfortunes have marked him
physically; he looks prematurely aged, but
his face is undaunted, noble, sad. The
modeling of that face is subtle and vigorous.
Rarely has any artist painted with such
penetration and intensity the expression
of his own inner life.

REMBRANDT VAN RIJN
(1606–69)

The Sampling Officials of the Drapers' Guild
or *The Syndics of the Cloth Guild*

Oil on canvas, 75¹/₄ × 109⁷/₈"
Signed and dated in stipple letters on the
tablecloth: Rembrandt. f. 1662
Lent by the City of Amsterdam

Toward his old age, Rembrandt's technique
gained in power and directness. His brush
stroke became broad and vibrant. *The
Sampling Officials* shows his art as a
portrait painter at its highest. The sitters
were members of a board of inspectors of
dyed cloth. With complete assurance
and naturalness Rembrandt has captured
them as they gather round their meeting
table. The portraits have marvelous
individuality, yet the cohesion of the group
as a whole is perfect. All eyes are centered
on the spectator, who is captivated and
drawn into their circle. The sober black and
white of the men's garments is boldly set
off by the rich oriental rug on the table and
by the light that falls on the faces and
on the wainscoting from the high windows
out of sight to the left.

REMBRANDT VAN RIJN
(1606–69)

The Bridal Couple or *The Jewish Bride*

Oil on canvas, 47⁷/₈ × 65¹/₂″
Signed lower right: Rembrandt. f. 16
Probably painted after 1665
Van der Hoop Collection, lent by the
City of Amsterdam

At the end of Rembrandt's life stand some of the summits of his art. He painted his last works triumphantly, using now his brushes, now the palette knife, now his fingers. His colors become more magical, more plastic, than ever before. *The Bridal Couple* is compounded of such magic, its splendor of red and gold intensified by the gleam of high impastos. The composition and coloring suggest that Rembrandt may have thought of Venetian examples.

The spell cast by the painting derives not so much from its colors, however, as from the expressions of infinite tenderness on the faces of the young man and his bride. The light touch of their hands is the ultimate caress.

It is uncertain whether this painting is a portrait of Jewish neighbors of Rembrandt, or whether, while being a portrait, it represents at the same time a biblical story, such as that of Isaac and Rebecca. Some observers have seen in the man's face a resemblance to Titus, Rembrandt's son, who was married in 1668 and died a few months later, aged twenty-seven.

Attributed to
CAREL FABRITIUS (1622–54)

The Beheading of John the Baptist

Oil on canvas, 58⅝ × 47⅝"
Probably painted about 1641–43

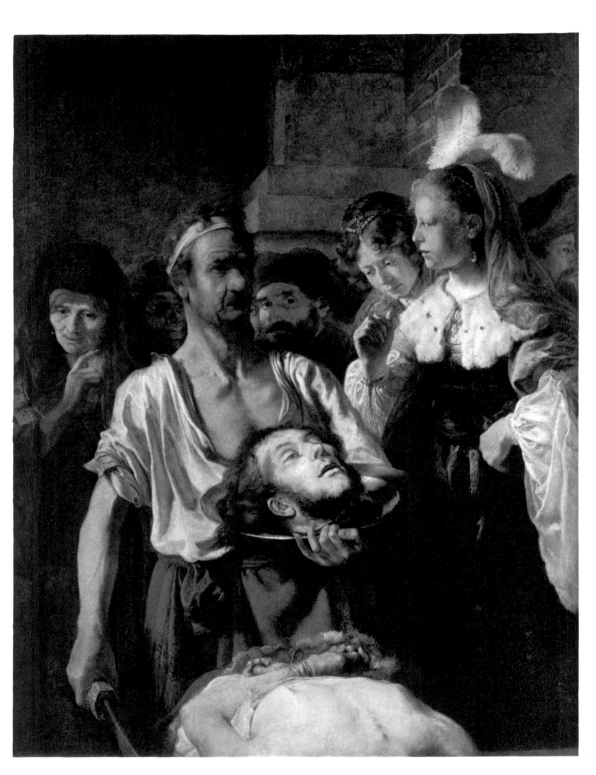

Throughout his life Rembrandt had many
pupils, although the numbers dwindled
after his bankruptcy and removal from his
big house on the Breestraat. As early as
1628 the young Gerrit Dou came to his
studio in Leiden, and in 1660 Aart de
Gelder was his last pupil. Carel Fabritius
studied under him about 1641. It is not
possible, however, to form an accurate
picture of the working methods of
Rembrandt's studio, which must have been
very large during his prosperous years.
Did the pupils assist in Rembrandt's own
paintings? Did he correct their work to
make it more salable? Did various pupils
work on one canvas? Whatever occurred,
the standards of the time were different from
those of today.
The question must therefore remain
unresolved just who in Rembrandt's studio
was responsible for this painting, whether
one pupil or several, and how much
any one may have had as his share. The
conjecture has arisen because of the varying
quality in the execution of the figures.
The background figures are weak, whereas
the executioner, his face tanned by the sun,
is beautifully painted, as is the white-
skinned Salome. The attribution to
Fabritius is based in part on mention of a
Beheading of John the Baptist by him at a
sale in 1687.

GOVERT FLINCK (1615–60)

Isaac Blessing Jacob

Oil on canvas, 46¹/₈ × 55¹/₂"
Signed and dated upper right: G. flinck 1638

In Protestant Holland religious paintings were not for churches but for private homes. Everyone knew the Bible stories and their moral meanings. For Rembrandt the Scriptures were an abundant source of inspiration. His imaginative interpretation of biblical themes was an example for his pupils. Flinck was twenty-three and just out of the master's studio when he painted this dramatic episode of the aged Isaac and young Jacob. Rembrandt's influence is evident, but the vivid coloring shows Flinck's original talent.

FERDINAND BOL (1616–80)

Elisabeth Bas

Oil on canvas, 46¹/₂ × 36″
Probably painted 1635–40

Now and then one of Rembrandt's pupils
equaled the master himself, and it
becomes difficult to tell the work of the one
from the other. Such was the case with this
superb portrait of an old woman—Elisabeth
Bas (1571–1649), widow of Admiral
Jochem Hendricksz. Swartenhout.
Exhibiting many of the qualities of
Rembrandt's portraits from his first
Amsterdam years, this painting was long
admired as a Rembrandt. Analysis of the
brushwork makes it apparent now that an
attribution to Bol is more reasonable.

FERDINAND BOL (1616–80)

*Four Governors of the Amsterdam Leper
Asylum*

Oil on canvas, 7′ 4¹/₄″ × 10′ 2″
Signed and dated on a book: f. Bol fec. 1649
Lent by the City of Amsterdam

In addition to the depiction of civic-guard
companies, another form of group portrait
became popular in the seventeenth century—
that of the governors or governesses of
charitable institutions, or of guild officials.
The demands that such a commission
made on a painter were undoubtedly not so
heavy as those of the civic-guard pieces,
where a much larger number of persons had
to be immortalized on canvas, but the lesser
commission was difficult enough.
The governors were usually portrayed
sitting around a table with the symbols of
their functions, such as a moneybag,
an account book, writing material, before
them. Often a servant stands in the
background. In this painting Bol has added
a warden of the asylum, who brings in a
little boy with an infected head. This bit of
action animates the scene, making this
governors' piece more memorable than
other paintings treating similar subjects.

NICOLAES MAES (1634–93)

An Old Woman Saying Grace
or *Prayer without End*

Oil on canvas, 52³/₄ × 44¹/₂"
Signed at right, on tablecloth: N: M: S:
Painted about 1655
Lent by the City of Amsterdam

Nicolaes Maes, a pupil of Rembrandt in
1648, was one of the many artists who at
first felt the master's strong impact and
later went on to develop styles of their own.
His predilection was for portraits and
genre subjects, frequently single figures of
women at their work or mothers nursing
a child. In *An Old Woman Saying Grace* he
has beautifully expressed the moment of
spiritual communion and peace. A warm,
strong light shines on the woman and on
all the homely, familiar objects about her.
Time seems suspended—save for the cat,
whose own prayer seems about to be
answered.

GERRIT DOU (1613–75)

Self-Portrait

Oil on oak, 18⁷/₈ × 14¹/₂″
Painted about 1645

In 1628, when he was about fifteen years old, Gerrit Dou began studying with the twenty-two-year-old Rembrandt in Leiden, and remained with him until 1631, when the older artist went to Amsterdam. Rembrandt, as he matured, painted ever more broadly, whereas Dou became more precise and specialized. Yet in his Leiden years Rembrandt paid close attention to detail, and his influence on his young pupil is quite in line with his early style. Dou was a successful artist. During his lifetime his paintings were greatly appreciated and commanded high prices.

In his *Self-Portrait* Dou pictures himself leaning out of an arched window smoking his pipe, a book in front of him. A painter's easel and a boy busy grinding paint are just visible in the room behind. Pinned to the window ledge, below the book, is a piece of paper with his name on it, just as Jacob Cornelisz. signed his self-portrait in 1533 (see plate 19).

Following the seventeenth-century fashion of screening paintings with a curtain, Dou presents this little picture as a painting within a painting. The green curtain at the right hangs ready to be pulled shut at any moment, blocking the scene inside from curious eyes. Thus the artist heightened the *trompe l'œil* effect, so dear to his day and age.

ADAM PYNACKER (1622–73)

The Shore of an Italian Lake

Oil on canvas mounted on wood,
38³/₈ × 33⁵/₈″

Signed lower left: APijnacker

Pynacker, who spent three years in Italy, belongs to the group of Italianizers of whom Johannes Both (see plate 61) was the most important representative. In *The Shore of an Italian Lake* his personal interpretation of Claude Lorrain's influence shows clearly in the strong contrast between the dark, shadowy foreground and the sun-drenched mountain ridge in the background. Unlike most of the Italianizers, however, Pynacker's colors are more often cool than warm; the greens usually shade into blues, and the skies are clear. His well-drawn people and animals have an important place in the composition.

61

JOHANNES BOTH (c. 1618–52)

Italian Landscape with Artists Sketching

Oil on canvas, 73⁵/₈ × 94¹/₂″
Signed at right, on a rock: JBoth. f
Van der Hoop Collection, lent by the
City of Amsterdam

Italy attracted Dutch artists in the seventeenth century, as it did artists of all countries, and many of them, upon returning home, perpetuated the strong impressions they had received south of the Alps. Thus a school of painters of the classical and pastoral landscape developed parallel to the large group of more realistic painters of Dutch scenery. The Utrecht master Both was the chief representative of the Italianate trend.

In its romantic conception of nature, his *Italian Landscape* shows the influence of Claude Lorrain. Beside a mountain stream, in the golden light of late afternoon, shepherds and travelers converse with artists sketching beside the road.

MICHIEL SWEERTS (1624–64)

A Painter's Studio

Oil on canvas, 28 × 29¹/₈"
Painted about 1650

Sweerts, who was born in Brussels and
ended his life as a missionary in Goa, spent
many years in Rome, where he was
apparently in touch with the international
group of artists who specialized in the
representation of Roman popular life.
His studio interior shows a master and his
pupils at work in the penumbra, painting
from a nude model or drawing from
antique sculpture. A silvery light drifts
down from the high window and falls on
the fantastic cluster of sculptural fragments.

63

GERRIT ADRIAENSZ.
BERCKHEYDE (1638–98)

The Flower Market at Amsterdam

Oil on canvas, 17³/₄ × 24"
Signed on a boat: Gerrit Berck Heyde
Van der Hoop Collection, lent by the
City of Amsterdam

In 1612 Amsterdam launched a vigorous
expansion program. During the course
of the century the three great semicircular
canals girding the old town were dug,
and handsome buildings went up all over
the city. The largest and finest was the
new Town Hall on the Dam, built in
1648–62 and proudly hailed by the Dutch
as the Eighth Wonder of the World. Many
artists recorded Amsterdam's beauties,
among them Gerrit Berckheyde of
Haarlem, who specialized in townscapes.
Here he views the rear of the massive Town
Hall as it looms over the houses along the
stretch of the Nieuwe Zijds Voorburgwal
where the flower market was held.

JACOB ISAACKSZ.
VAN RUISDAEL (1628/29–82)

The Mill at Wijk bij Duurstede

Oil on canvas, 32⅝ × 39¾″
Signed lower right: JV Ruisdael
Painted about 1670
Van der Hoop Collection, lent by the
City of Amsterdam

This landscape is one of the most
impressive of the Dutch school. The
human figures in it are dwarfed by the lofty
sky and towering clouds. In the gray light
the mill rises dramatically on the bank of the
Rhine River, thrusting out its wings against
the approaching storm. Although this
mill no longer exists, another closely
resembling it makes the scene today in
Wijk bij Duurstede much as Ruisdael saw it.
The ruins of the Bishop's Palace, in the
right background, and the church are still
there.
Jacob van Ruisdael, the best known of a
family of painters, gained fame in his
lifetime for his solemn and sometimes
melancholy landscapes, which celebrate the
majesty of nature. His sense of
monumentality in landscape is unique
among Dutch painters. Ruisdael was born
and spent his early years in Haarlem, but
after 1656 lived in Amsterdam. He studied
medicine at the University of Caen, receiving
a degree in surgery there in 1676.

AERT VAN DER NEER
(1603/4–77)

River Scene by Moonlight

Oil on oak, $21^5/_8 \times 40^1/_2''$
Signed lower center with initials

The entire scale of light effects in landscape,
from dawn till dusk and in all seasonal
changes, was familiar to Dutch painters.
Some had a predilection for moonlight
scenes; such was Aert van der Neer, whose
second speciality was winter landscapes.
He revealed great skill and feeling for
atmosphere in dealing with the problems of
painting twilight. When day's colors have
faded, only the reflection of the pale sky
and the light of the rising moon remain.
His palette in this moonlit river scene is
therefore virtually reduced to brown and
silvery tones. Van der Neer's interpretation
of evening has a wonderful stillness. As man
and animal prepare to retire for the night,
the translucent shadows slowly settle
over the riverbanks.

JAN STEEN (1626–79)

The Prince's Birthday

Oil on oak, 18¹/₈ × 24⁵/₈"
Signed on the piece of paper, at the end of
inscription: JSteen
Probably painted about 1660

Jan Steen was one of the most imaginative
of Dutch artists. His masterly
characterizations of middle-class life attest
his narrative talent as well as his technical
brilliance. The people in his canvases move
about as on a stage, talking, making
gestures, bringing expressive action to the
scene. Here he shows us a gay moment
in a tavern. The kneeling man, with a
dagger in one hand and a glass in the other,
toasts the health of young Prince
William III of Nassau. The high-spirited
man answering the toast is probably the
artist himself.
Jan Steen was born in Leiden and died
there. He worked in The Hague, Delft
(where he ran a brewery), Warmond, and
Haarlem. In 1672 he returned to Leiden,
where he owned an inn. His first wife was
the daughter of Jan van Goyen.

JAN STEEN (1626–79)

The Sick Lady

Oil on canvas, 29⁷/₈ × 25″
Signed upper right: JSteen
Painted about 1665
Van der Hoop Collection, lent by the
City of Amsterdam

Steen was an expert draftsman, deftly
handling small groups and crowded
compositions with equal ease. He was also
an exceptional colorist. As a storyteller,
he loved to point a moral with a humorous
twist. The doctor's visit to the ailing lady,
a theme he frequently painted, illustrates an
old saying: "Every cure is here in vain—
she suffers naught but love's great pain."
The spectator is made part of the silent
play by the feverish smile with which
the pretty girl asks for sympathy.

68

JAN STEEN (1626–79)

The Adoration of the Shepherds

Oil on canvas, 20⁷/₈ × 25¹/₄″
Signed lower left: JSteen
Painted about 1670

Jan Steen's religious paintings are less well
known than his genre pictures but no less
characteristic of his work. Moreover, they
belie his traditional reputation of having
been as profligate as some of the roisterers
in his tavern scenes. Only a man of deep
religious feeling could have handled biblical
themes as he does.
His particular power lies in his ability to
interpret these themes in terms of his own
time and place. With unabashed reverence
he places the Christ Child in a seventeenth-
century Dutch stall and transposes the
shepherds into everyday farmers and
their wives, bearing homely gifts to the
newborn Babe. One brings a cock,
another a tune on a bagpipe, a third a
bundle of faggots for the fire under the pot
of milk. Old Joseph gratefully doffs his
cap to a woman offering him a bowl of
eggs. And in the center, close to Mary
tenderly displaying her Child, is the donkey
who had shared in the whole miraculous
adventure.

69 and 69a

JAN STEEN (1626–79)

The Feast of St. Nicholas

Oil on canvas, 32¹/₄ × 27³/₄″
Signed lower right: JSteen
Painted about 1660–64

The feast of St. Nicholas on December fifth
still forms a high point in Dutch family life.
Children place their shoes by the hearth
for the candy and gifts—often dolls or toy
animals—the good saint will leave for them.
But woe to the child who has been
naughty. Instead of presents, he receives a
whip of twigs.
In this painting Jan Steen depicts the
St. Nicholas festivity. The little girl in the
foreground beams with joy and clasps
all her gifts tightly in her arms. Her big
brother apparently has been a bad boy,
for an older sister mockingly holds up his
shoe with a switch in it. However, the
grandmother in the background winks
reassuringly at him, no doubt to signal that
things are not hopeless and that behind
the bed curtain something better awaits him.
Only Jan Steen, with his technical mastery
and obvious love for children, could paint
such a scene so enchantingly, so full of
playful humor—and good things to eat when
the storm has blown over.

PAULUS POTTER (1625–54)

Horses in a Field

Oil on oak, 9¹/₄ × 11³/₄"
Signed and dated on the gate: Paulus Potter,
f 1649
Van der Hoop Collection, lent by the
City of Amsterdam

Cattle and horses in the lush meadows of the
flat Dutch countryside were the object of
Paulus Potter's constant love and attention
throughout his short life. By patient study
and self-restraint he came to be the master
of Dutch animal painting. Mingled with
his sober realism is a sensitivity to the
mellow tones of pastures and skies on a
summer day. He made this fine small panel
when he was twenty-four.

71 and 71a

JOHANNES VERMEER (1632–75)

The Kitchenmaid

Oil on canvas, 17⁷/₈ × 16¹/₈″
Painted about 1658

Vermeer is no storyteller; the action in his
paintings, if present at all, is of the simplest
type. He concentrates exclusively on the
variations of light in space and on the
surfaces of things. With rare and
admirable purity he communicates pictorial
feelings. Under his hands a commonplace
subject, such as this maid pouring milk, can
assume wonderful intensity. Her statuesque
figure has classical beauty, rounded and
made luminous by the gradation of tones
on the wall behind her. Typical of Vermeer
is the harmony of blue and yellow, each
color enhancing and reflecting the other.
The master's technical originality can be
seen in the surface modeling of the objects
on the table, where tiny dots suggest the
scintillation of light.

JOHANNES VERMEER (1632–75)

The Little Street

Oil on canvas, 21³/₈ × 17³/₈"
Signed lower left, on house wall: I V Meer
Painted about 1658

With a wife and eleven children to support,
Vermeer should have been a prolific artist,
but he was not. Each of his paintings, in
which every detail is perfect, must have
cost him months if not years to complete.
To supplement his income, he became a
picture dealer, without success. He died, in
debt, at the age of forty-three.
Vermeer never left his native Delft, and only
on rare occasions did he turn away from
his customary interior scenes to paint views
of the town. From the back of his house
on the Grote Markt, he could see, across the
street, the brick gables of the Old Men's
Home and the neighboring Old Women's
Home, depicted here to the right and left
of the alleyway. The painting is as unique
in composition as it is in pictorial treatment.
Behind a magical harmony of subdued
reds, olive greens, and creamy whites is a
calculated rhythm of geometrical planes.
These buildings were torn down in 1660 to
make way for the new hall of St. Luke's
Guild, of which Vermeer was a member.
Perhaps he knew they were to be
demolished and decided to record forever a
scene that must have been very dear to him.

JOHANNES VERMEER (1632–75)

The Letter

Oil on canvas, 17³/₈ × 15¹/₄"
Signed on the wall, left: IV Meer
Painted about 1666

The scene of *The Letter* is simple, the subject almost banal, but what wealth the painting contains! By the subtlest of calculations the artist has created a spellbinding illusion of depth. The composition is boldly divided into three vertical zones. The elements in the two foreground sections—the door to the left and the chair and curtain to the right—are so close we can almost touch them. It is as if we were poised on the threshold of the sunlit inner room containing the two women caught in an exquisite moment of suspended animation. The lute makes no sound, but there is music in the tonal chord of the ultramarine and rich yellow skirts. Shining like a star in the optical center of the picture is the luminous pearl of the lady's eardrop.

ADRIAEN VAN OSTADE
(1610–85)

Travelers Resting

Oil on oak, 14¹/₈ × 11³/₄″
Signed and dated lower left: Av. Ostade. 1671

Adriaen van Ostade, an excellent figure
painter, specialized in peasant scenes.
His figures are always farm men and women
resting in front of an inn or farmhouse,
or dancing and making merry. The peasant
at work is a subject that seldom appears in
seventeenth-century art.
Nearly all of Ostade's paintings are small,
but his fine craftsmanship permitted him
to make the most of his limited space.
His scenes are lively and unrestrained, with
many delightful details. He lived all his
life in Haarlem, where he was a pupil of
Frans Hals, but apparently was influenced
more directly by his fellow pupil,
Adriaen Brouwer.

GABRIEL METSU (1629–67)

The Sick Child

Oil on canvas, 13¹/₈ × 10³/₄″
Signed at the top of the map: G. Metsue
Painted about 1660

The people in Metsu's interiors are more important than their surroundings. The artist's humanity is clearly evident in this sensitive little canvas, painted with clear transparent colors reminiscent of Vermeer. But it is more than refined taste and technical perfection that makes this painting one of Metsu's masterpieces. By the intensely touching expression and languid attitude of the suffering child he establishes an emotional bond with his subject that is rarely found in seventeenth-century art.

PIETER DE HOOCH (1629–c. 1683)

Interior with Mother and Child
or *Maternal Duty*

Oil on canvas, 20⁵/₈ × 24″
Signed right, on the child's chair: Pr d'hooch
Painted about 1660

In no country was painting of interiors for the sake of portraying home life so popular as in seventeenth-century Holland. The Dutch cultivated their houses assiduously, and even the homes of plain people were well kept. De Hooch excels in this subject. With a fine feeling for perspective, he here represents a modest dwelling. Light is the living element. It enters from the sunny garden through the half-open door of the vestibule and glides into the room beyond, where it mingles with the gleam from the high window. Absorbed in arranging her child's hair, the mother does not notice the little dog, which seems to be gazing wistfully at the freedom of the out-of-doors. Serenity and calm happiness reign in this cosy interior.

GERARD TER BORCH (1617–81)

A Company in an Interior

Oil on canvas, 28 × 28³/₄″
Painted about 1653–55

In the eighteenth century this painting was
called *Paternal Admonition*, for it was
assumed that the girl with bowed head
was being reprimanded by her parents.
At some later date more astute observers
took a closer look at the picture and
discovered that the man with the sword was
not shaking a fatherly finger but holding
up a gold coin. The effect of this gesture on
the young lady can never be fathomed;
her face is hidden forever. The third person
present, the woman in black sipping from
a wineglass, appears to be keeping herself
apart. What is the significance of the coin,
the wine, the bed in the background? An
upper-class assignation, perhaps? To
Ter Borch and his contemporaries the
meaning must have been clear enough, but
to us it remains obscure.
Without knowing exactly what it is all
about, we can nonetheless derive endless
pleasure from the painterly qualities of this
interior scene. The man's elaborately
ornamented uniform is skillfully painted.
Yet the greatest attraction is the beautiful
material of the girl's dress. In Ter Borch's
time, as now, this figure made a strong
impression and was copied by such artists
as Philips Wouwerman, Pieter de Hooch,
and Caspar Netscher.
Gerard ter Borch was born in Zwolle. His
father, a tax collector who also drew and
painted, gave him his first lessons. Later he
studied with Pieter de Molijn in Haarlem.
After extensive travels in England,
Germany, Italy, Spain, and France, he
returned to his native land and worked
primarily in Deventer and Zwolle.

WILLEM KALF (1619–93)

Still Life

Oil on canvas, 28¹/₈ × 24³/₈″

While earlier still-life painters frequently arranged their material before a light background, Kalf obtained strong contrasts by doing the opposite. Against the obscurity of a vaguely defined space shine the metallic luster of gold and silver, the cool glaze of blue china, and the glowing hues of oranges and lemons. The embossed tankard resembles the work of the silversmith Christiaan van Vianen. Like several of his colleagues, Kalf was an art dealer as well as a painter. After a sojourn in Paris from 1640 to 1645, he returned to Amsterdam, where he lived the rest of his life.

BARTHOLOMEUS VAN DER HELST (1613–70)

Princess Mary Henriette Stuart

Oil on canvas, 78¹/₂ × 66⁷/₈"
Signed and dated upper left: Bartholomeus
van der helst. 1652. f.

Van der Helst and Rembrandt were contemporaries and fellow residents of Amsterdam, yet a greater contrast between two painters is difficult to imagine. Nothing of the power and humanity of Rembrandt's portraits can be found in Van der Helst's work. He depicted his subjects soberly and matter-of-factly, but with a craftsmanship so amazing and so in the taste of the time that it is no wonder he was one of the most celebrated portraitists of the seventeenth century. In the eighteenth and nineteenth centuries he was often valued more highly than Rembrandt.

The invitation to paint Mary Stuart (1631–60), widow of the Stadholder William II, Prince of Orange, was undoubtedly the most distinguished of the innumerable commissions that fell to him. He portrayed the princess seated on a silver chair and clad in a silvery white satin gown. In her hand she holds a large orange, an allusion to the House of Orange. Through the arched window at the left is a view on the Buitenhof at The Hague from the Stadholder's quarters, with the tower of St. Jacob's Church in the background. This portrait gave the painter ample opportunity to display his technical virtuosity.

ABRAHAM VAN BEYEREN
(1620/21–90)

Still Life

Oil on canvas, 49⅝ × 41¾"
Signed with monogram below the niche

Van Beyeren, like so many other seventeenth-century painters a specialist, limited himself to riverscapes and still lifes—still lifes with fish or with flowers, and especially still lifes that display a wealth of gold- and silverwork, glass, Chinese porcelain, fruit, flowers, and food. As in this painting, he customarily arranged all these things on a table covered with a velvet cloth. For background, he was fond of a niche or a window.

Although a lesser artist would have been unable to unify such a superfluity of material, Van Beyeren was a painter of remarkable talent. Using fairly broad strokes, paying meticulous attention to each object, but never lapsing into too great detail, he painted in many colors. Yet his paintings are not in the least gaudy. It is as if the whole were bound by a light that glides softly over the objects, leaving some in a half-dusk and revealing others in their delicate beauty. Among this abundance, which is conceivable only in the full glory of a century of prosperous, sensuous burghers, the artist nearly always painted a clock, symbol of the transiency of beauty and worldly riches.

81

JOHANNES VAN DE CAPPELLE
(1626–79)

Winter Scene

Oil on canvas, 20¹/₄ × 26¹/₂″

The Amsterdammer Johannes van de Cappelle was a wealthy man. By profession a cloth-dyer, he taught himself painting on the side. There would thus be every reason to call him an amateur were it not that his work ranks among the best produced in the seventeenth century. He possessed a large art collection, including drawings by Hendrick Avercamp and by the seascape painter Simon de Vlieger, and paintings by Rembrandt, Brouwer, Rubens, Seghers. Van Dyck, and Jordaers. In his own painting he limited himself primarily to sea- and beachscapes and to winter landscapes. Originally his work was greatly influenced by Simon de Vlieger; later he seems to have been particularly attracted to Rembrandt's work.

EMANUEL DE WITTE
(c. 1617–92)

Interior of a Gothic Church

Oil on canvas, 48 × 41″
Painted about 1680–82
Van der Hoop Collection, lent by the
City of Amsterdam

Among the many Dutch architectural
painters, De Witte alone conveyed the idea
that his church interiors were in daily use,
both for religious services and other
activities, such as entombments. At the same
time he captured the stately grandeur of the
spacious naves, using high lights and deep
shadows to form strong contrasts. Often a
figure in the foreground, seen from the
back, helps to create the sense of height
and distance characteristic of his art. In this
painting he combined elements from the
Old Church and the New Church in
Amsterdam.

MEINDERT HOBBEMA (1638–1709)

A Watermill

Oil on oak, 24³/₈ × 33⁵/₈″
Signed lower left: M. Hobbema
Van der Hoop Collection, lent by the
City of Amsterdam

Together with Ruisdael, Cuyp, and Van
Goyen, Hobbema was one of the
Netherlands' leading landscape painters. A
friend and pupil of Jacob van Ruisdael, he
sometimes went with his master into the
country to paint. But Hobbema's vision was
more cheerful than Ruisdael's. He depicted
cottages and watermills amid sunlit trees,
delighting in the varying greens of foliage
moving in the wind. Usually he introduced
a few small figures to enliven the scene.

JAN VAN DER HEYDEN
(1637–1712)

The Dam in Amsterdam

Oil on oak, 26³/₄ × 21⁵/₈"
Signed on the canopy of the Weighhouse:
VHeyde
Lent by the City of Amsterdam

Jan van der Heyden made a name not only
as a painter of townscapes but also as a
mechanical engineer. Among other things,
he improved street lanterns and fire-
fighting equipment. His technical talent is
strongly evident in his paintings, which
nearly always contain buildings accurate in
architectural detail and perspective. But
Van der Heyden was also a lyric painter,
letting his imagination roam at will over his
surroundings, and often combining views
of various places or buildings in one
painting.
In painting the Dam in Amsterdam, the
great square at the heart of the city, the
artist was fascinated primarily by the New
Church with its irregular but majestic
architecture. Sunlight skims in a play of
light and shadow along the façade at the
northwest corner of the Dam. At the left a
portion of the Town Hall (today the Royal
Palace) is visible, and to the right the
Weighhouse, torn down in 1808 by Louis
Napoleon. Van der Heyden's style of
painting had great influence on the
topographical painters of the eighteenth
century.

WILLEM VAN DE VELDE
THE YOUNGER (1633–1707)

The Harbor of Amsterdam

Oil on canvas, 5′ 10³/₄″ × 10′ 4³/₈″
Signed and dated on piece of driftwood,
right center: w. v. velde J 1686
Lent by the City of Amsterdam

The Van de Velde family counted many
painters. Willem van de Velde the Elder was
a marine painter of note. His namesake son
and pupil, also a specialist in ships and naval
battles, surpassed him in artistic importance.
Both father and son received frequent
commissions from the States General, and
both went later to England to paint for
the English court. They were present at
many of the naval engagements of their time.
This large and stately canvas shows the
Amsterdam harbor crowded with ships and
craft of numerous types. The large
man-of-war flying the Dutch colors is the
Golden Lion, flagship of Admiral Cornelis
Tromp. It is being saluted by a state yacht.
The scrupulous accuracy in all details of
the ships' structure and rigging in no way
detracts from the admirable handling of the
total scene. The cloud-filled sky is in itself
a masterpiece.

CORNELIS TROOST
(1697–1750)

Family Group in an Interior

Oil on canvas, 37 × 32^1/$_2$"
Signed and dated lower right: C. Troost 1739

Although Dutch painting declined in importance in the eighteenth century, a small number of artists maintained the high standard of technical brilliance set by their predecessors. They excelled especially in portrait painting, conversation pieces, and floral still lifes. Troost was renowned for his portraits and humorous scenes. His wit has been compared with Hogarth's, but he was never satirical. The influence of French styles on clothing and interior decoration shows clearly in this *Family Group*, and there is also a new sweetness in the elegant poses and smiling expressions.

JAN VAN HUYSUM (1682–1749)

Flowers

Oil on oak, 31⁷/₈ × 24″
Signed and dated lower left: Jan Van Huysum
fecit 1723

A passion for exact imitation and the most
sustained detailing was evident in Dutch
painting at the end of the seventeenth
century and continued into the eighteenth.
Jan van Huysum's floral pieces mark one
of the high points of this perfectionist style.
In contrast to many other painters of
flowers, he worked directly from nature
and not from drawings made earlier.
Here he has painted a luxuriant bouquet of
summer flowers in a brown earthenware
vase decorated with a relief depicting the
infancy of Bacchus. The drops of water on
the petals, the bird's nest with eggs, the
little insects—ants, butterflies, beetles—are
painted so perfectly they almost deceive the
eye. Van Huysum had great influence.
Until well into the nineteenth century
flower painters used his work as a model.

PIETER GERHARDUS VAN OS
(1776–1839)

A Canal in 's-Graveland

Oil on canvas, 43³/₄ × 35¹/₄"
Signed and dated lower center:
PG van Os f. 1818

Art did not flourish in the Netherlands of
the late eighteenth and early nineteenth
centuries. Nevertheless, from time to time a
painting was created which, because of its
originality or simplicity and spontaneous
artistry, rose above the stiff and uninspired
efforts of most painters of that period.
Pieter Gerhardus van Os, son of the flower
painter Jan van Os, rarely produced work
above the average. In this view of the
village of 's-Graveland near Hilversum,
however, he excelled most of his
contemporaries. By painting from a high
point of view, as it were, he achieved a new
and fresh approach to the Dutch landscape.

89

PIETER RUDOLPH KLEYN
(1785–1816)

The Park of Saint-Cloud

Oil on canvas, 39 × 51¹/₈"
Signed and dated lower left: P R Kleyn 1809

During the French occupation from 1795 to
1813, artistic life in the Netherlands became
dispirited. To encourage greater activity
the King of Holland, Napoleon's brother
Louis, instituted stipends for art students.
One of the beneficiaries was young Pieter
Rudolph Kleyn, who went to Paris and
studied with Jacques-Louis David. Wounded
in the battle of Quatre-Bras, preceding
Waterloo, he died a year later. The
remarkable view of Saint-Cloud, one of his
very rare works, has surprising clarity and
freshness. It is an exceptionally fine example
of the classicist style imposed on the
Dutch sensibility for landscape.

WOUTER JOANNES VAN TROOSTWIJK (1782–1810)

The Raampoortje at Amsterdam

Oil on canvas, 22¹/₂ × 18⁷/₈"
Signed and dated right, on the embankment:
wjvan Troostwijk 1809

During the seventeenth and eighteenth centuries the subjects chosen for townscapes were almost always important buildings, streets, or canals, giving the work a topographical character. In this painting, perhaps for the first time, the emphasis is on the picturesque. The artist was attracted by the play of the white snow against the dark canal embankment and by the dusky curves of the little gate and bridge. Against the misty background the huge tower of the West Church is visible only as a shadow. Wouter van Troostwijk is little known. He died when he was twenty-eight, a year after he painted this canvas.

91

JOHANNES JELGERHUIS (1770–1836)

The Bookshop

Oil on canvas, 18⁷/₈ × 22⁷/₈"
Signed and dated on a rafter:
I: Jelgerhuis Rz 1820

The actor Johannes Jelgerhuis was also an artist of modest talent; in this painting he outdid himself. Light streams through the large windows and open door into the spacious bookshop of Pieter Meyer Warnars, on the Vijgendam in the heart of Amsterdam. Books are tidily arranged on high bookshelves; two bareheaded bookdealers attend to a customer, while their hatted clerk works behind the partition to the right; the street outside is filled with life. Jelgerhuis avoided heavy shadows and let light tones prevail. His painting gives an impression of the way in which French classical ideals were adapted by Dutch artists.

ANTON MAUVE (1838–88)

Morning Ride along the Beach

Oil on canvas, 17³/₄ × 27¹/₂″
Signed lower right: A. Mauve f
Probably painted about 1880

Anton Mauve was an important member of
the Hague School of Impressionists that
flourished in the last quarter of the
nineteenth century. Although Impressionism
did not reach the heights in the Netherlands
that it attained in France, Dutch artists
gave their own special interpretation to it.
In Mauve's *Morning Ride* the atmosphere
and mood of a sunny summer morning is
brilliantly conveyed. Primarily a landscape
artist, he was drawn to the coastal area
with its dunes and beaches, the ever-varying
aspects of the sea, the people of the fishing
villages, and the holiday visitors.

PAUL JOSEPH CONSTANTIN
GABRIEL (1828–1903)

In the Month of July

Oil on canvas, 40¹/₈ × 26″
Signed lower left: Gabriel f.
Painted shortly before 1889

Gabriel studied under Barend Cornelis
Koekkoek (1803–62), a landscape painter
highly respected in his time. Nothing of
the teacher's careful, Romantic style is
reflected in the pupil's mature work,
however. Like Mauve, Gabriel joined the
Hague School and thereafter devoted
himself entirely to Impressionist painting.
He worked a great deal in the vicinity of
Amsterdam, where he probably painted
In the Month of July. The windmill—of the
North Holland type—is reflected in the
canal into which it pumps water from the
lower-lying polder in the background. But
the mill is not the subject of the painting.
As the title makes clear, the theme is July,
the month of full and glorious summer.

94

GEORGE HENDRIK BREITNER
(1857–1923)

The Bridge over the Singel at the Paleisstraat,
Amsterdam

Oil on canvas, 39³/₈ × 59⁷/₈″
Signed lower left: G. H. Breitner
Painted 1893–98

Apart from his contemporary, Vincent van
Gogh (who left the Netherlands for
France), Breitner is today considered the
strongest personality among Dutch artists of
the latter half of the nineteenth century.
He was the painter of Amsterdam street life
and town views, and of portraits and nudes
as well. This important picture well
illustrates his method of animating a
composition: the foreground figure
advances literally into the spectator's arms,
and the strong play of diagonals in the
other planes reinforces the sensation of
movement. The brushwork is a combination
of vehement and delicate strokes, expressive
of distances near and far.

PIERO DI COSIMO (1462–1521)

Giuliano da Sangallo

Oil on oak, 18³/₄ × 13¹/₄″
Painted about 1505

An eccentric, and a great artist, Piero di Cosimo is one of the most interesting personalities in the brilliant Florentine art world of the late Renaissance. Portraits are exceptional in his work, which consisted mainly of mythological fantasies and religious subjects. With almost Flemish love for detail and landscape, he sharply modeled this portrait of Sangallo and a companion picture of his father, Francesco Giamberti, also in the Rijksmuseum. The biographer Vasari admiringly wrote that the two portraits seemed almost alive. Sangallo, a noted Florentine architect and friend of Michelangelo's and Raphael's, was employed by Pope Julius II for the building of St. Peter's in Rome.

96

CARLO CRIVELLI (c. 1430–c. 1495)

Mary Magdalene

Oil on poplar, 59⁷/₈ × 19¹/₄″
Signed on a strip of paper lower right:
Opus Karoli. Crivelli Venet
Painted about 1475

Among the small group of early Italian paintings in the Rijksmuseum, this panel is one of the most noteworthy. The Venetian Crivelli, who worked for a long time in the Marches, isolated from the main currents, has a characteristic linear style. There is a lavish abundance of beautiful detail in his work, enhancing its monumentality. Swathed in her sinuous mantle, her blonde hair flowing down, Mary Magdalene rises before a golden background. Her delicate elegance is almost oriental.

JACQUES BLANCHARD (1600–1638)

Irene and Her Maids Tending the Wounded Sebastian

Oil on canvas, 60¹/₄ × 80″
Probably painted about 1637

The rescue of Sebastian is a less frequent theme in art than his martyrdom. According to the *Acta Sanctorum* of the saint, Sebastian did not die of his wounds, but was nursed back to life by a devout woman, Irene. In this painting Blanchard depicts Irene, left, and her maids as they remove the arrows from the young martyr's body. The artist's second wife, whom he married in 1637, may have served as model for Irene. The picture's monumental construction and large areas of color are characteristic of the Baroque trend gaining ascendancy in the early seventeenth century.
A Parisian, Blanchard studied for a time in Italy and worked in Bologna, among other places. Upon his return to Paris he soon established a high reputation as a painter, but death brought his promising career to an early end.

98

GIOVANNI BATTISTA TIEPOLO
(1696–1770)

Telemachus and Mentor

Oil on canvas, 43¹/₄ × 28³/₈″
Painted about 1740

Famous alike for his large decorations in palaces and churches and for his refined sketches, Tiepolo embodies the resplendent last phase of Venetian Baroque art. His compositions have sweeping movement, his colors are chimerical. In this picture he illustrates an episode from the story of Ulysses' son Telemachus, whose adventures had become popular in the eighteenth century through François Fénelon's epic, *Télémaque*. Armed with a bow and carrying his father's heavy quiver, the youth sets out to slay his mother's suitors, urged on by Mentor.

FRANCISCO JOSÉ
DE GOYA Y LUCIENTES (1746–1828)

Don Ramón Satué

Oil on canvas, 42¹/₈ × 32⁷/₈"
Signed and dated lower left: D. Ramon Satue,
Alcalde de Corte, Pr. Goya 1823

Daring in its simplicity and directness, this
portrait is one of the finest the great
Spanish painter executed in his old age.
The model stands before us self-assured,
his pose informal, a look of indomitability
on his passionate face. The luminous red
of his waistcoat lends fiery accent to the
severe black and white of his other garments.
Don Ramón is intensely alive. A mayor of
Corte and a judge in Madrid, he was,
like Goya, a liberal antimonarchist in
post-Napoleonic Spain. When menaced by
the persecutions of the new regime, Goya
sought refuge in the house of Don Ramón's
uncle. The artist was then seventy-six.
A few months later he fled to France.

JEAN-ÉTIENNE LIOTARD
(1702–89)

View from the Artist's Studio at Geneva

Pastel on parchment, 17³/₄ × 22⁷/₈"
Signed on back: Vue de Genève du Cabinet
peinte par Liotard

Landscape was an unusual theme for
Liotard. Looking out of his studio window
toward the fields and mountains around
Geneva, he made this unconventional
picture. In his hands pastel became a
wonderful medium for rendering even the
transparencies of distant shadows. The wide
valley lies glowing under the radiant sky.
To the left, with the vineyard in his little
garden behind him, the painter represented
his cheerful self in profile.

Drawings and Prints

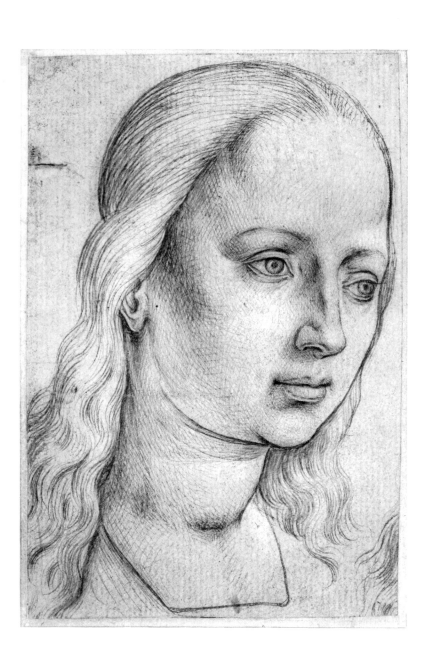

Attributed to
HUGO VAN DER GOES (c. 1440–82)

Head of a Young Woman

Silverpoint drawing, 6 × 3³/₄″

Drawings by the fifteenth-century masters of the Low Countries are very rare. Whether done after a model or a painting, this delicate, precisely modeled head shows a splendid technique. The fine silverpoint gives not only great purity of line but also the softest gradation of tones. The drawing is attributed to Hugo van der Goes, the most powerful Ghent painter in the period after Jan van Eyck.

102

MASTER OF THE
AMSTERDAM CABINET
(active last quarter of fifteenth century)

The Idolatry of King Solomon

Drypoint, diameter 6¹/₈″

The most important collection of engravings by this unknown artist, who worked mainly in the Middle Rhineland, is in the Rijksmuseum Print Room. For that reason he is called "Master of the Amsterdam Cabinet," although he is also referred to as "Master of the Hausbuch," from the book of his drawings in the Waldburg-Wolfegg Collection in Germany. He has a remarkably lively style and an unusual drypoint technique. With eloquent acuteness he here represents the story of the aging King Solomon induced by one of his seven hundred exotic wives to worship false gods.

103 and 103a

LUCAS VAN LEYDEN
(c. 1489–1533)

The Return of the Prodigal Son

Engraving, 7 × 9⁵/₈"
About 1510

In this engraving the versatile Lucas reveals
his originality and technical perfection.
The scene of the Prodigal Son's homecoming
is set in a luminous landscape. In the
foreground the haggard wanderer kneels
before his old father, watched by the
wondering onlookers. Far away to the right
appears a miserable episode from his
earlier adventures: he feeds himself from
a pig trough.

JACQUES II DE GHEYN
(1565–1629)

The Farm

Pen drawing, 7⁵/₈ × 12¹/₄″
Signed and dated lower center: J Gheyn. in 1603.

The De Gheyn family, like so many others, fled the Spanish occupation of their native Antwerp to settle in the Northern Netherlands. Jacques studied under his father, a glass painter, but is best known for his drawings and paintings. This elaborate drawing reveals his Mannerist style combined with an accurate observation of nature and love for realistic detail. He made a copper engraving after this same subject. Interest in the aspects of rural life became lively at the beginning of the seventeenth century.

ROELANT SAVERY (1576–1639)

The Monkey

Chalk and brush drawing, 16 × 11³/₄″
Signed lower left: R Savery

Another of the many Flemish artists who fled to Holland, Savery specialized in painting landscapes with animals. Here he sympathetically observes a forlorn little monkey, imprisoned by his chained collar. The sensitive play of chalk and watercolor brings out the glossy coat. Between 1604 and 1615 Savery worked in Prague and Vienna as court painter to Emperor Rudolf II, and the monkey may have been a court pet.

JAN VAN GOYEN (1596–1656)

The Dunes near Scheveningen

Black chalk and brush drawing, 7$^{1}/_{8}$ × 10$^{5}/_{8}$"
Signed and dated: VG 1649

Most of Van Goyen's numerous landscape drawings are black chalk sketches, some of which seem to have been done on the spot. He developed a characteristic cursory style in this medium: energetic signs, rapidly noting the forms, and soft tonal gradations, creating admirable effects of light and of aerial perspective.

JACOB ISAACKSZ.
VAN RUISDAEL (1628/29–82)

The Oak in the Forest

Etching, 7$^{1}/_{8}$ × 10$^{5}/_{8}$"
Signed in lower margin: Ruisdael f.

No one has expressed better than Jacob van Ruisdael the romantic beauty of weather-worn oaks, battered by storms but still erect, near pools in solitary woods. This etching is a splendid example of such a dramatic vision of nature. There is a strong suggestion of light and color in the refined distribution of gray tones of varying intensity.

REMBRANDT VAN RIJN
(1606–69)

Christ with the Sick around Him
or *The Hundred Guilder Print*

Etching, 11¹/₈ × 15¹/₂″
Completed in 1649

The most famous of Rembrandt's etchings is commonly called *The Hundred Guilder Print* because he is supposed to have bought it back for that amount at an auction, where it did not sell. The artist combined etching and drypoint to achieve a superb gradation of tones and contrasts in the print. The composition is elaborate, treating several themes of Christ's ministry. The Messiah heals the sick, blesses the children, and admonishes His disciples. His face in his hand, the rich young man meditates Christ's profound words. This etching powerfully reveals Rembrandt's deep feeling for suffering humanity and his unmatched talent for expressing inner life.

REMBRANDT VAN RIJN
(1606–69)

The Woman at the Door

Pen drawing, 9¹/₈ × 7″

Rembrandt experimented tirelessly with
pen, brush, and chalk. In thousands of
drawings, from rapid sketches to careful
studies, he exercised his hand, noting down
reality or giving free play to his
imagination. The theme of women and
children particularly fascinated him. In this
example, from his middle period, his pen
moved quickly, capturing shapes, attitudes,
and expressions with nervous strokes.
The old woman, drawn with such
affectionate observation, bears some
resemblance to the artist's mother.

110

REMBRANDT VAN RIJN
(1606–69)

Jan Six's Bridge

Etching, 5¹/₈ × 8³/₄″
*Signed and dated lower right: Rembrandt
f. 1645*

In Rembrandt, the etcher equaled the
painter and the draftsman. As long as his
eyes were good enough for the exacting
task of etching, he often preferred this
medium above all others. He made about
three hundred plates, covering the widest
choice of subject matter and showing
amazingly diverse modes of expression.
This sunny view of a little country bridge
looks as airy as a pen sketch. Rembrandt's
contemporaries related the tale that he
made the plate at Jan Six's country house,
winning a wager against his friend that he
could complete the etching before the return
of a servant, sent to the village to fetch
some mustard.

REMBRANDT VAN RIJN
(1606–69)

Portrait of Shah Jahân

Pen and brush drawing, 2⁵/₈ × 2³/₄″

This drawing is one of a series that
Rembrandt made after Indian miniatures of
the Moghul period (seventeenth century)
in his own collection. His careful use of
brown ink and brown wash on tinted
Japanese paper has produced a delicate,
oriental effect.

112

REMBRANDT VAN RIJN
(1606–69)

Reclining Nude

Brush drawing, 5¹/₄ × 11¹/₈″

A magnificent late drawing, *Reclining Nude*
belongs to a group of studies Rembrandt
made from a nude model. Done entirely
with the brush, it is a real painter's
drawing. The apparently casual strokes set
down the essential and nothing more.
Yet there is a wonderful modulation of
light values intermingled with shadow
accents. The diagonal composition suggests
space and depth.

JEAN-ANTOINE WATTEAU
(1684–1721)

Studies of a Woman's Head

*Pencil, red and black chalk, and brush
drawing, 9 × 13⁷/₈″*

Watteau's delightful study sheets may be
said to contain the essence of the French
spirit. As this drawing demonstrates, he
combined sharp realistic observation with
elegance of line. The application of black
and sanguine chalks in sensitive, nervous
strokes produces a charming effect of
blended colors. Watteau made use of such
studies from nature in several paintings.
This rosy beauty, here seen from different
angles and in graceful attitudes, appears in
various of his works, among others in a
Fête Galante in the Dresden Gallery.

JEAN-HONORÉ FRAGONARD
(1732–1806)

The Umbrella Pines of the Villa Pamphili

Pencil and brush drawing, $17^5/_8 \times 13^1/_4{}''$
Drawn about 1773–74

During his years in Rome, Fragonard made
several superb drawings of the umbrella
pines at Villa d'Este in Tivoli and at the
Borghese and Pamphili villas. With an
almost Impressionist touch he here renders
the play of light and shadow in the
spacious park, where, under the
monumental arch of trees, people gaily
converse and amuse their children. The
artist's mastery of chiaroscuro is well shown
in his treatment of the tree trunks and
foliage.

Sculpture

MASTER OF JOACHIM AND ANNE
(active about 1460–80)

Joachim and Anne at the Golden Gate

Oak, height 18¹/₄"

The unknown sculptor has been
provisionally named after this group. Most
extant medieval Dutch sculptures are wood
carvings that formed part of larger
retables. Nearly all were originally colored,
but the polychrome coating has frequently
disappeared. With a firm sense of
three-dimensional form, the sculptor of
Joachim and Anne cut and chiseled the
hard block of wood into the spiritualized
figures of the pious couple who have heard
that at last a child will be born unto them.
This child will become the Virgin Mary.

NORTH-NETHERLANDISH
SCULPTOR (c. 1500)

The Flight into Egypt

Polychromed oak, height 41³/₄″

By Dutch standards, this relief-like group is large. Its charm derives from the winning candor of the execution, which harmonizes sweetly with the touching subject of the young mother with her baby—Mary with the Infant Christ—riding a patient donkey.

ADRIAEN VAN WESEL
(c. 1420–1500)

Music-Making Angels and St. Joseph

Oak, 17¹/₂ × 14³/₄″

Only recently has the name of the creator of
this group been discovered. A prominent
sculptor, he was actively employed in
several Dutch towns, but mainly in Utrecht.
His speciality was large altarpieces. The
group is a fragment of an Adoration from
such an altar. The treatment of the faces,
the flowing garments, and the wings reveals
how this late Gothic artist mingled realistic
tendencies with traditional stylization.

HENDRICK DE KEYSER
(1565–1621)

Bust of a Man

Polychromed terra cotta, height 24³/₈″
Dated 1606

In the Northern Netherlands, sculpture did
not flourish in the seventeenth century,
the Golden Age of painting. Lack of native
talents and scarcity of stone and marble
deterred the growth of a sculptural
language. Nevertheless, a few masters
produced excellent works. De Keyser was
architect and master sculptor of the
municipality of Amsterdam. His colored
terra-cotta portrait shows his able modeling
and the realism of his style, which is
typically Dutch.

ARTUS QUELLINUS
(1609–68)

Prudence

Terra cotta, height 35⁷/₈″

For the decoration of their magnificent new
Town Hall, the Amsterdam magistrates
called in the Antwerp sculptor Quellinus.
Under his direction the building was
embellished inside and out with numerous
reliefs and statues. This terra-cotta sketch
for one of the large bronze figures on the
roof is a good example of his style, in which
the splendid surface modeling harmonizes
with the general monumental outline.

ROMBOUT VERHULST
(1624–98)

Bust of a Woman

Terra cotta, height 17³/₄″

Decorative naturalism is the mark of
Verhulst's portraits in terra cotta, which
seem to have been modeled directly from
life. These pieces illustrate the artist's
sensitivity and almost pictorial handling of
light and shadow. Verhulst came to the
Netherlands from Malines and, like
Quellinus, worked on the Amsterdam Town
Hall. He received commissions from all
parts of the country for funeral
monuments. This bust probably portrays
Maria van Reygersbergh (1628–73), wife of
Willem Baron van Liere, lord of
Oosterwijk and the two Katwijks.

ANTWERP SCULPTOR

Virgin and Child

Ivory, height 22⁷/₈"
About 1700

In the last quarter of the seventeenth
century, sculpture in Antwerp attained a
refinement admirably exemplified by this
ivory statue. Mary with the Child is
portrayed standing on a crescent moon,
crushing Satan in the form of a dragon.
This popular motif derived from the
Renaissance. The tender grace of the Virgin
evinces an unusual craftsmanship and a
highly cultivated taste. The work is
tentatively attributed to Artus Quellinus the
Younger (1625–1700). For an ivory piece,
it is exceptionally large.

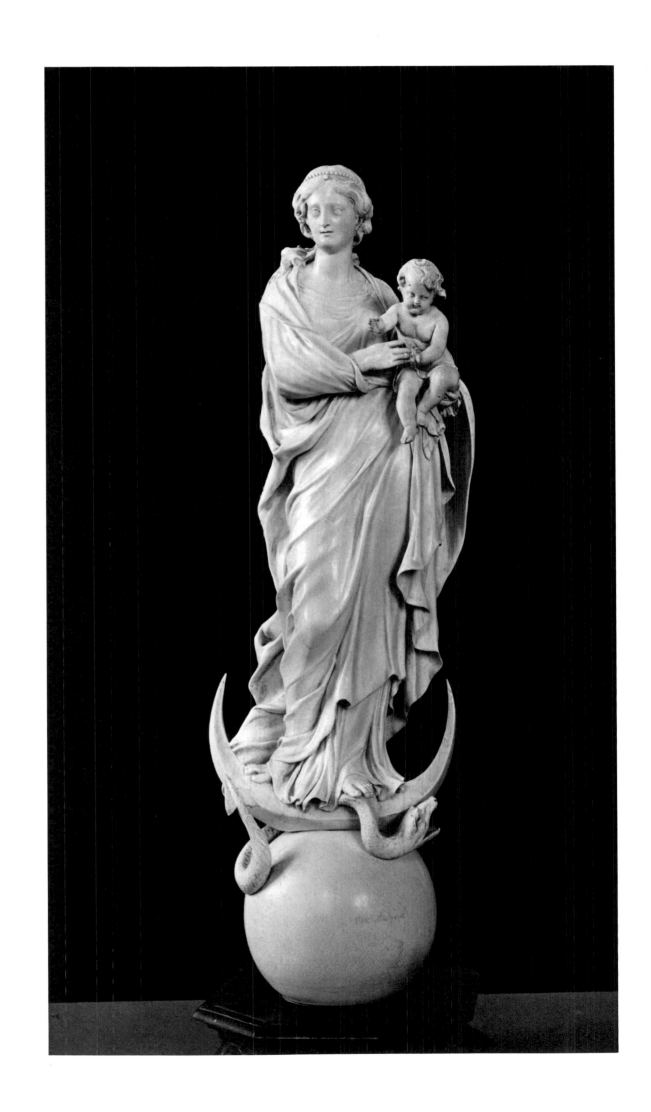

ÉTIENNE-MAURICE FALCONET
(1716–91)

Seated Figure of Cupid

Marble, height 34¹/₄"
Dated 1757

Falconet was one of the most celebrated
Parisian sculptors of the second half of the
eighteenth century. When he was eighteen
years old, he entered the studio of Jean-
Baptiste Lemoyne; in 1745 he made his
debut at the Paris Salon. In 1757,
presumably upon the recommendation of
Madame de Pompadour, he was appointed
artistic chief at the Sèvres factories.
Catherine II of Russia invited him to
St. Petersburg in 1766 to make a large
monument in memory of Peter the Great.
Falconet carved this little statue of Cupid,
known as *L'Amour menaçant*, at the
command of Madame de Pompadour for
her Château de Bellevue. It was so dearly
loved in the eighteenth century that other
artists made copies after it, some of which
still exist. The plaster model was exhibited
in 1755 at the Paris Salon.

Silver, Jewelry, and Glass

AMSTERDAM CRAFTSMAN

Drinking Horn of the Arquebusiers Guild

Buffalo horn mounted in silver, height 14³/₄″
Made in 1547
Lent by the City of Amsterdam

Drinking horns of this type were used at the banquets of the guilds and stored in their treasuries. This elegant specimen belonged to the group of civic militia, the Kloveniers, for whom Rembrandt later painted *The Night Watch*. It is a fine example of the late-Gothic transition style and one of the early pieces bearing the Amsterdam mark. The lion and dragon on the footpiece are the heraldic animals of the Van der Schelling family.

124 and 124a (following page)

PAULUS VAN VIANEN
(c. 1570–1613)

Oval Dish with the Story of Diana and Actaeon

Silver, 16¹/₈ × 20¹/₂″
Dated 1613

A member of a Utrecht family of silversmiths and in his day a famous and much-traveled artist, Paulus van Vianen worked for ten years at the pomp-loving court of Emperor Rudolf II at Prague. In his finely embossed and sculptured silverwork he masterfully combined figurative and ornamental motifs, following the international style of late Mannerism. This large dish has reliefs on two faces, as does a jug that completes the set. Both pieces are decorated with stories of Diana. The scene on the front of the dish represents Diana surprised by Actaeon; that on the back, the death of Actaeon.

ADAM VAN VIANEN
(c. 1569–1627)

Pedimented Drinking Bowl

Silver, height 6¹/₈″
Dated 1621

Paulus van Vianen's brother Adam brought
to full development a typically Baroque
ornamental style, in which human, animal,
and vegetable motifs intermingle in fluid
movement. The richness of the material is
accentuated by asymmetrical curved forms,
which create a multitude of bright
reflections on the sinewy metal surface. This
style has been called "lobar design."

JOHANNES LUTMA THE ELDER
(c. 1584–1669)

Two Salt Dishes

Partly gilded silver, height 9¹/₂″
Marked Amsterdam, with the letter H
indicating 1639

Each of these salt containers rests on a three-sided, fancifully lobed footpiece, which supports the figure of a cherub holding the daintily formed, shell-like dish. The footpieces and dishes are gilded, the figures plain. This pair must have belonged to a series, for two similar pieces are now in the Amsterdam Historical Museum, and others probably existed. Evidence for this assumption is found in the portrait of Lutma (see plate 127) by the Amsterdam artist Jacob Adriaensz. Backer (1608–51). The salt container in the painting is somewhat different from the four known examples. Since Lutma posed with this piece, he must have considered it among his important works. It has sometimes been held that early seventeenth-century Dutch silver was never gilded. These salt dishes, and that in the portrait, prove otherwise.

JOHANNES LUTMA THE ELDER
(c. 1584–1669)

Ceremonial Pitcher and Basin

*Silver, pitcher height 8¹/₄″, basin diameter
23³/₄″*
Dated 1655
Lent by the City of Amsterdam

Lutma was the chief silversmith in
seventeenth-century Amsterdam. Most of
his works are masterpieces of the lobar
style, but in this admirably proportioned set
the forms are simple and functional, and
the decoration is restrained. All the elegance
of curve and countercurve goes into the
handle, styled like a sea serpent. The set
was commissioned for the solemn
inauguration banquet of the Amsterdam
Town Hall in 1655.

AMSTERDAM SILVERSMITH

Scalloped Plate

Chased silver, diameter 17³/₄"
Signed with master's mark: G.B.
Made in 1661

After the middle of the seventeenth century
the style of Dutch silver changed, a flower
design replacing the lobar ornament. The
unknown craftsman who made this plate
seems almost to express the struggle
between the old and new styles. He used
lobar ornaments to frame the plate,
drawing them back into the borders and
depths of the scallops. The rounded
segments he decorated with an abundance
of chased flower tendrils and *putti*. In the
center of the plate he placed a pastoral scene.

ANDELE ANDELES (1687–1754)

Coffee Urn

Chased silver, height 16¹/₂″
Dated 1729

The style of the French court was
introduced into the Netherlands primarily
through the influence of Daniel Marot
(c. 1660–1712), a French architect in the
service of Stadholder William III. Both in
form—derived directly from a garden urn—
and in ornamentation, this coffee urn is a
beautiful example of the way in which the
Louis XIV style was adapted to Dutch
silver. By a rhythmical alternation of plain
and ornamented patterns, the Frisian
silversmith Andele Andeles succeeded in
giving the piece a monumental character.
Its eighteenth-century owners added a dash
of cinnamon to the coffee they poured
from it.

GERMAN JEWELERS

Pendant with Cimon and Pera

Gold, enamel, pearls, rubies, and other
precious stones, height 4³/₄"
About 1600

Renaissance jewelry reflects the splendor of
that period's taste and fashion. Imaginative
craftsmen took advantage of the bizarre
shapes of large, irregular Baroque pearls to
create animal forms such as this spirited
cockerel. Others incorporated finely
enameled figures into their designs. All the
pieces display their makers' and owners'
delight in the artful blending of sparkling
material and fanciful form.

Toothpick

Gold, enamel, turquoise, and other precious
stones, height 2⁵/₈"
About 1600

Cockerel Brooch

Baroque pearl, gold, enamel, rubies, and
other precious stones, height 3"
Second half of the sixteenth century

WILLEM VAN HEEMSKERK
(1613–92)

Marriage Dish with Diamond Engraving

Glass, diameter 12¹/₂″
Dated 1685

Italian craftsmen introduced the art of glass blowing into the Netherlands toward the end of the sixteenth century. Soon the Dutch ovens produced glass of good quality, and glass decorators—often amateurs— developed the technique of engraving with a diamond. The Leiden cloth merchant and poet Willem van Heemskerk was the major specialist in the field of calligraphic glass-engraving. He probably made this handsome marriage dish for his son.

ITALIAN CRAFTSMEN

Dragon-Shaped Vase

*Rock crystal with gold and enamel,
height 14¹/₈″
About 1650*

At the princely courts of Europe in the sixteenth and seventeenth centuries, vessels cut in semiprecious stones and in rock crystal were much in vogue. In Italy the Milanese rock-crystal cutters were especially famous for their exquisite craftsmanship and fantastic inventions. After the patient operations of grinding, cutting, engraving, and polishing had been completed, goldsmiths finished the work with finely enameled gold mountings. In this fabulous beast, the sparkle of the costly crystal is intensified by the festive ornamental incisions.

DUTCH GLASS ENGRAVER

Rummer with Diamond Engraving,
"The Siege of Damietta"

Glass, height 8¹/₂″
Made in 1644
Lent by the Royal Society of Antiquarians

This is a fine example of the engraved
rummer. The decoration stands out lightly
against the pale green of the glass. The scene
commemorates a glorious feat of arms
by the Frisian and Dutch Crusaders,
who in 1218, after long and heavy fighting,
took the Egyptian city of Damietta from
the Saracens. For centuries this epic was
popular in the Netherlands, especially
among the people of Haarlem.

Ceramics

DELFT POTTERY

Tile Picture

Earthenware, 66¹/₂ × 35⁵/₈″
About 1700

Pottery was a characteristic national craft
in seventeenth- and eighteenth-century
Holland, and Delft became one of the most
important ceramic centers in northern
Europe. The success of imported Oriental
porcelain led the Dutch to attempt to
produce fine china at home. Although
unable to bake hard porcelain, the Delft
manufacturers succeeded in making
excellent earthenware, famous for its
painted decorations in blue, but also
produced in many other colors. According
to the kind and number of colors used, the
tiles had to undergo several firings. Painted
tiles were especially popular for wall
adornment, whether mounted as borders,
fireplace backings, or decorative panels.
In this large panel, flowers, birds, and
insects are tastefully combined.

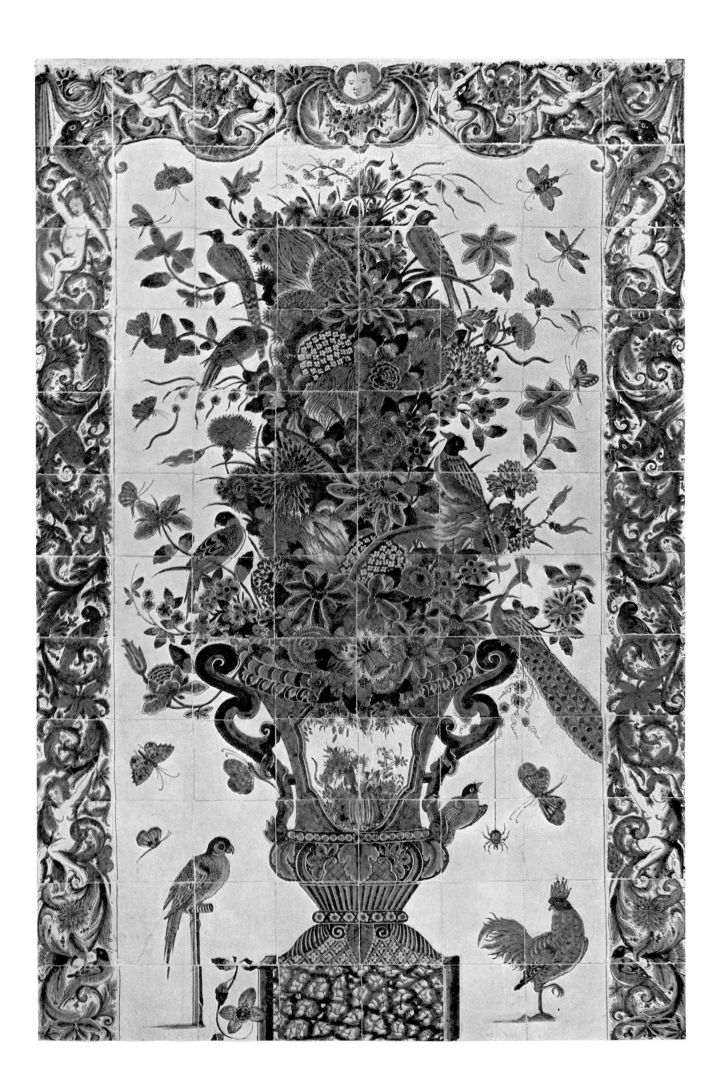

DELFT POTTERY

Tulip Vase

Earthenware, height 42¹/₂″
Lent by the Royal Society of Antiquarians

An exceptional piece of blue and white
delftware, this tulip holder in the form of a
ziggurat is built of ten superposed water
compartments, each a separate vase with
four spouts. When filled with tulips, one in
each spout, the tall pyramid creates an
extraordinarily decorative effect.

PIETER ADRIAENSZ. KOCX
(died 1703)

Ewer with Basin

*Polychrome and gilt delftware, ewer height
16″, basin height 10¹/₄″*
About 1700

Eastern porcelain became so popular that
Dutch potteries attempted to reproduce not
only the material but also the decorative
designs. Painters of delftware were adept at
imitating Chinese and Japanese patterns.
This rare set, marked PAK for Pieter
Adriaensz. Kocx's important factory called
The Greek A, is decorated in red, blue, and
gold, following the style of Japanese Imari
porcelain. The painter clearly did not copy
his model; instead, he translated the
Asian motif into a typically Dutch idiom.

138 and 138a

Painted by
JOHANN GREGORIUS HÖROLDT
(1696–1775)

Vase

Meissen porcelain, height 18¹/₂″
About 1727

Founded about 1710, the Meissen factory
during the first ten years of its existence
produced much red stoneware and
white porcelain, the latter usually
ornamented with designs in relief. The
pottery, then under the direction of Johann
Friederich Böttger, achieved little initial
success with painted porcelain. A change
came about only with the arrival, in 1720,
of Johann Gregorius Höroldt, a master
porcelain-painter.
This graceful ornamental vase was made by
the factory for its patron, Augustus the
Strong, Elector of Saxony. Höroldt, who had
replaced Böttger as director, painted the
refined scene with Chinese figures. The
group on the lid has been ascribed to the
modeler Johann Gottlieb Kirchner. The
piece is a good example of the way in which
oriental and occidental themes were
combined.

MEISSEN FACTORY

Vase

Porcelain, height 13³/₄"
About 1725

Augustus the Strong was an avid collector
of Chinese porcelain, and to suit his taste
the Meissen factory, in the early years
of Höroldt's leadership, followed Chinese
designs. This vase, one of a pair, is painted
in colors over a bluish-white underglaze.
Although the images are skillfully depicted,
they show little understanding of the ideas
behind Chinese landscape painting, the
original source of inspiration.

140

Model by
JOHANN JOACHIM KÄNDLER
(1706–75)

Harlequin Group

Meissen porcelain, height 6¹/₄"
About 1740–45

A few years after Höroldt became director
of the Meissen factory, the sculptor
Johann Joachim Kändler was appointed
chief modeler. For nearly four decades the
two artists worked together, bringing
Meissen porcelain to its highest peak.
Kändler achieved much success with figures
from Italian *commedia dell'arte*. This group
shows Columbine with a child and a
violin-playing Harlequin. Another
Harlequin—a standing figure with a goblet
—once stood behind Columbine, but has
been lost. The painting of this piece, above
all the dark brown skirt decorated with
flowers in many colors, is particularly free.

LOOSDRECHT POTTERY

Chocolate Jug

Porcelain, height 6³/₄″
Signed: M.O.L.
About 1774–82

Owing to increasing competition, chiefly from English factories, Dutch porcelain works lost ground in the eighteenth century. They were not successful economically, and their production was small. Nonetheless, some of the potteries turned out excellent pieces. From the Loosdrecht factory near Amsterdam, directed by a church minister named De Mol, came this simple chocolate jug with its charming decoration of shells, a lizard, and a spider and a wasp in mortal battle.

Textiles and Furniture

FRANS SPIERING
(1551–1621 or 1630)

Tapestry: Niobe's Pride and Punishment

Wool and silk, 11′ 9³/₄″ × 17′ 4³/₄″
Made in 1610

Flemish weavers brought the art of tapestry weaving to the Netherlands when they settled in Dutch towns after the fall of Antwerp in 1585. Prominent among these craftsmen was Frans Spiering, who set up a successful workshop in Delft. One of his celebrated series represented episodes from the story of Diana. This tapestry, magnificently designed and aglow with sumptuous colors, narrates a tragic scene. Niobe, proud of her numerous offspring, advances from the left and tries to prevent the Theban women from honoring the statue of Latona, whom she despises for having borne only two children. But these children, the mighty gods Apollo and Diana, cruelly avenge their offended mother. They are depicted in the background, killing all the Niobids with their darts. Nor does Niobe herself survive the disaster: inconsolable, she weeps herself to death and is turned into a stone from which flow eternal tears.

GOBELIN FACTORY, PARIS

Tapestry from the series "Amours des Dieux"

Wool and silk, 12' 3⁵/₈" × 7' 8¹/₂"
Made in 1784

Against a crimson background surrounded by rich Louis XVI motifs of flower garlands and festoons hangs a medallion with a picture of Eros, symbolizing natural science. In his raised hand the infant god holds a burning glass with which he has lighted the torch in his other hand. The subject of this medallion was taken from François Boucher. Maurice Jacques designed the borders of the tapestry, enlivening them freely with many kinds of birds and two small dogs, which stare impudently from their pedestals.

The execution of the series *Amours des Dieux*, to which this tapestry belongs, was entrusted to Jacques Neilson, a director of the Gobelin factory from 1776 to 1784. This specimen from the well-loved and frequently repeated series was presented by Louis XVI to Prince Henry of Prussia in 1784. The earliest series, with different borders, was woven in 1748.

ITALIAN LACEMAKER

Man's Collar

Reticella needlepoint lace, width 13³/₄"
Made about 1600–1620

Expensive lace embellishments were high
fashion at the beginning of the seventeenth
century. Some of the finest early
needlepoint came from Italy. This rare
complete specimen of a man's collar, with
its wonderful line and varied geometrical
pattern, must once have been its owner's
pride.

145

NORTH-NETHERLANDISH
CABINETMAKERS

Credence or Treasure Cabinet

Oak, 57⁷/₈ × 40³/₄ × 29¹/₄"
Made about 1525
Lent by the Royal Society of Antiquarians

This exceptional piece of late Gothic
furniture was probably made for a guild of
civic archers in Alkmaar to hold their
treasure—ceremonial badges and
implements, silver dishes and beakers—
which were displayed on special occasions.
The cabinet is decorated on all four sides
with fine tracery-work panels separated by
carved pilasters. The piece was thus
designed to stand in the middle of a room.
In its general form it is architectural; in its
ornamental details it resembles a shrine.

NORTH-NETHERLANDISH CABINETMAKERS

Cushion Cabinet

Palisander on oak frame,
89¹/₈ × 98 × 33⁷/₈″
Made in 1689

From the middle of the seventeenth century, the two-doored cupboard was an important element in the Dutch interior. Because of the "cushions" on the door panels, a piece like this is called a cushion cabinet. Designed after classical architectural motifs and proportions, it is Baroque in its plastic effect and by virtue of the costly material used. This cupboard has palisander (Brazilian rosewood) veneer and ornamental carvings on an oak frame. It bears the arms of the Alberda family of Groningen.

NORTH-NETHERLANDISH FURNITURE MAKER

Chair

Palisander, height 43³/₄″
First half of the seventeenth century

Most Dutch furniture was made of oak prior to the seventeenth century, but, as the middle classes prospered, costly exotic woods came more and more into fashion. This delicately designed and richly sculptured chair is made of Brazilian rosewood, its decorative parts of ebony.

DUTCH CRAFTSMEN

Margaretha de Ruyter's Dollhouse

Wood, 78³/₄ × 55¹/₈ × 22"
About 1675

The style in which wealthy Dutch burghers of the last quarter of the seventeenth century furnished their homes is reflected faithfully in this magnificent dollhouse, which belonged to a daughter of Admiral de Ruyter. Such houses were not really playthings for children but objects for collectors, who delighted in the artistic miniature reproduction of the things of everyday life.
On the ground floor of this house, from left to right, are the cellar, the kitchen, the dining room; on the middle floor, the bedroom and the drawing room; on the top floor, the peat loft, the linen room, and the nursery. Each room has its own furnishings, complete with beautiful silver, glass, and china, and the whole reveals a high level of craftsmanship. The original dolls, finely modeled in wax, are dressed in the latest fashion.

NORTH-NETHERLANDISH
FURNITURE MAKERS

Bedstead

Pine, $141^3/_4 \times 76^3/_4 \times 88^5/_8''$
End of the seventeenth century

In 1685 the French architect Daniel Marot
(1663–1752) came to the Netherlands to
work on various Orange residences. He did
much to cultivate the Dutch taste for
French styles, and under his influence
Dutch furniture making reached an
international level. Although none of the
state beds designed by him and manufactured
in the Netherlands can be identified with
certainty, this example clearly shows his
touch. It is draped with plain and cut
velvet, presumably of Italian make. The
bedstead derives from Castle Rozendaal in
Gelderland, where it was used for such royal
guests as Queen Mary Stuart, wife of
William III, Stadholder of the Netherlands
and King of England.

ABRAHAM AND DAVID
ROENTGEN

Writing Table

*Frame of oak, maple, and walnut, with
various veneers, $53^1/_8 \times 40^1/_2 \times 24^3/_8''$
About 1765*

This richly ornamented escritoire was made
for Johann Philipp von Walderdorf,
Elector of Trier, as is indicated by the
medallion portrait, the monograms, and the
coats of arms applied at various places.
Abraham Roentgen (1711–93) and his son
David (1743–1807) were among the best
German furniture makers of the eighteenth
century. In this relatively small piece they
attained unsurpassed wealth and variety
of ornamentation and a perfect execution of
the many drawers and drop-leaf panels.
The handsome marquetry, presumably made
by David Roentgen, is inlaid with rosewood,
ebony, palisander, and satinwood worked
with tortoise shell, mother-of-pearl, copper,
and bone. The side panels (see detail)
were inspired by prints by the Dutch
artist Nicolaes Berchem (1620–83).

Historical Collection

DUTCH TEXTILE WORKERS

Costume of a Herald, House of Orange-Nassau

Embroidered silk, length 35³/₄"
Made in 1647
Lent by the Royal Society of Antiquarians

This tunic was made for the funeral
procession of Stadholder Prince Frederick
Henry in 1647. The embroidered arms in the
four quarters are those of the House of
Nassau, and the escutcheon in the center
bears the arms of the House of Orange.
The costume was also used at the funeral of
Prince William II in 1650, and again a
hundred years later, in 1751, at the funeral
of Prince William IV.

152

Objects from the Novaya Zemlya
Expedition of 1596–97

Some of the straits and capes of the Arctic
islands of Spitsbergen and Novaya Zemlya
bear the names of Dutch seamen, keeping
alive the memory of a famous early
expedition. Sent out to find a northern
route to China, an Amsterdam ship under
the command of Willem Barents and Jacob
van Heemskerck became icebound in
August, 1596. The crew had to abandon
ship and endure the sufferings of the long
polar winter in a wooden hut they built on
Novaya Zemlya. After many adventures and
the death of Barents and others, the little
band of survivors reached home in the
autumn of 1597. Nearly three centuries
later, in 1871, the ruins of the hut were
discovered, along with a variety of supplies,
instruments, tools, household utensils,
maps, books, and Barents' diary, telling a
moving story of hardship and endurance.
The find is unequaled for the light it throws
on the equipment of the explorers of that
period.

WILLEM VAN DE VELDE
THE ELDER (c. 1611–93)

The Battle of Ter Heyde

*Three pencil sketches glued together to form
one long strip
Pen-and-ink painting on canvas, 5′ 7″ × 9′ 7³/₄″
Signed and dated lower left: W. v. velde f
A° 1657 d′galyoot van velde*

Painters of sea battles were set high
requirements by their patrons. The fighting
ships they depicted must be not only
clearly recognizable, but accurate in every
detail of structure and rigging. Battle order,
wind direction, and weather conditions
had to correspond with those of the battle
itself. The painter therefore had only one
recourse: to go along with the fleet.
Willem van de Velde, who did so, might
be called a seventeenth-century war
photographer.
These on-the-spot sketches and the painting
made from them depict the battle of
Ter Heyde, which took place on August 10,
1653, off the Dutch coast between
Scheveningen and the Hook of Holland.
In it the Dutch fleet under Maerten
Harpertsz. Tromp and Witte de With
fought the English fleet under George
Monk; Tromp was killed. The artist
was in the thick of the battle, busily
sketching from his galiot (see detail).
Van de Velde invented his own painting
technique. He drew the design with black ink
on a nearly white undercoat of oil paint,
only occasionally making use of a brush to
indicate shadows. His works are justly
called pen paintings. Other sea painters
following him also used this method.

155 and 155a

VLISSINGEN SHIPBUILDERS

Bow and Stern from Model of a Man-of-War

Length 15′, width 6′ 9″, height 12′ 11″
Built in 1698

This bow and stern are from a model, the largest and most complete of its kind, of a seventy-gun man-of-war. Built at Vlissingen for the Admiralty of Zeeland, the model was rigged under the personal supervision of Admiral Cornelis Evertsen. The greatest care was taken in executing the structural details, the splendid decorative carvings (done by C. Moesman), and the intricate rigging. The full model gives valuable information about the art of shipbuilding at the end of the seventeenth century.

ENGLISH SHIPBUILDERS

Stern Decoration from the "Royal Charles"

Carved wood, painted and gilded,
9' 1" × 12' 4³/₄"
Made in 1663

This stern decoration from the English flagship the *Royal Charles* is of exceptional historical and artistic importance. The splendid battleship, originally called the *Naseby*, was built in 1655. At the Restoration, King Charles II rebaptized it in his own honor and replaced the Commonwealth decorations with the royal arms. The ship was captured by the Dutch at Chatham, during a bold raid by Admiral de Ruyter's fleet on the Medway in 1667. The Dutch were so proud of their prize that they kept the ship as a curiosity in one of their ports. Even after the hull deteriorated, the stern was preserved. It is a monumental example of Baroque decoration.

FRANS POST (c. 1612–80)

Landscape in Brazil

Oil on canvas, 42¹/₄ × 67⁷/₈″
Signed and dated lower left, on a calabash:
F. Post 1662

An interesting chapter in the history of Brazil is the short period from 1636 to 1644 during which Count John Maurice of Nassau was governor of the Dutch possessions there. When he went to his new post, the count took along a number of artists and mapmakers, including the young painter Frans Post. During his eight years' stay in Brazil, Post painted landscapes and made drawings of the Dutch and Portuguese settlements. He was so impressed by the exotic beauty of the country that after returning to Holland he continued to paint Brazilian landscapes from his studies or from memory. Seventeen years after he reached home he made this imaginary panorama of the town of Olinda, near Recife. The building on the hill is the Franciscan convent. In the foreground, amidst the rich Brazilian vegetation, the artist represented with evident delight a group of exotic animals—an anteater, a sloth, an armadillo, monkeys.

Oriental Art

CHINESE SCULPTOR

Seated Bodhisattva

Polychromed wood, height 42¹/₈″
Twelfth century
Museum of Asian Art

No other deity has been as reverently
worshiped in the Far East as the
Bodhisattva Avalokitesvara—in Chinese,
Kuan-yin. This enlightened being is the God
of Mercy, whose compassion saves suffering
mankind. In this life-size statue he is
represented in the relaxed position called
"Royal Ease," his right arm stretched out
toward those who need help and
consolation. From this pose and from the
expression of exalted meditation emanate
sublime dignity and ideal calm. This
masterpiece of late Sung wood carving
preserves traces of the original color and
gold-leaf decoration, which lend mysterious
vivacity to the soft curves and deep hollows
of the modeling. The treatment of the figure
is remarkably realistic.

Attributed to
CEYLONESE SCULPTOR

Buddha

Bronze, height 16¹/₂″
About A.D. 600
Museum of Asian Art

Examples of the earliest Singhalese
Buddhist sculpture are extremely rare.
Although found in East Java, this slender
bronze figure probably comes from Ceylon.
The golden protuberance on the head, a
distinctive mark of the Buddha, may have
been added in Java. Despite its modest size,
the statuette has noble grandeur. The folds
of the robe, modeled in rhythmic lines,
drape the figure elegantly. The beautiful
ritual gesture of the right hand reassures the
faithful, that of the left indicates
argumentation.

160

HINDU-JAVANESE SCULPTOR

Head of Buddha

Andesite, height 12¹/₄″
Eighth century
Museum of Asian Art

The great temple of Barabudur in Middle
Java is considered the most important
Buddhist monument in greater India.
Innumerable stone statues and reliefs on the
temple's many galleries and terraces provide
a panorama of Buddhist hagiology.
Even a fragment like this head conveys an
idea of the majestic quality of that
sculptural ornamentation. In portraying
supreme spiritual serenity, the sculptor
attained plastic perfection.

SOUTH INDIAN SCULPTOR

Siva Natarâja (Siva as King of the Dance)

Bronze, height 61"
Thirteenth–fourteenth century
Museum of Asian Art

Of the South Indian bronzes the most
famous are those depicting the deity Siva as
dancer. Cast about 1300, the statue here
reproduced is considered by many to be
one of the handsomest pieces extant.
The dance of Siva, god at once of creation
and destruction, is not an ordinary but a
cosmic dance, symbolically expressing the
destruction of the universe and its
re-creation at the end of the world period
(Kalpa). Surrounded by a circle of flames
emanating from the mouths of two monsters,
Siva tramples the dwarf Evil under his right
foot. Neither the snake curling about his
forearm nor the flame on the palm of his
hand can harm him. His hair is spread out in
waving tresses, which serve as marks of
respect to India's seven holy rivers, out of
which the goddess of the Ganges emerges
to honor the sublime deity. The positions of
the hands and feet, the emblems held in the
hands, and the headdress all contribute to
the impressive symbolization of the
universe in motion.